About the Author

Robin Ratchford was born in the UK. He thinks it was collecting colourful stamps as a child that first sparked his interest in foreign lands and cultures. He has lived in six different countries and visited more than a hundred others and their territories. Robin has a background in international affairs, and travel, adventure and discovery are central themes in his life. He is currently based in Belgium, where he lives with his dog Mortimer.

FROM SOUK TO SOUK

FROM SOUK TO SOUK

Travels Through the Middle East

ROBIN RATCHFORD

Matador
9 Priory Business Park
Kibworth Beauchamp
Leicestershire LE8 0RX, UK
Tel: (+44) 116 279 2299
Fax: (+44) 116 279 2277
Email: books@troubador.co.uk
Web: www.troubador.co.uk/matador

ISBN 978 1783062 805

British Library Cataloguing in Publication Data.
A catalogue record for this book is available from the British Library.

Typeset in Aldine401 BT Roman by Troubador Publishing Ltd

Matador is an imprint of Troubador Publishing Ltd

Acknowledgements

With thanks to Ann, Eva and José for their help and support.

With thanks to James at Untamed Borders for having made the trip to Afghanistan possible.

"Possessed with the thought of travelling about the world of men and seeing their cities and islands."

– Sinbad the Sailor, Scheherazade

Contents

Preface

The Middle East fascinates me, not only because of its central role in the evolution of civilisation, but because of its pivotal position in contemporary geopolitics. Both aspects affect our everyday lives. In this part of the world, the links between the past and the present appear immutable, their hold on the future unbreakable.

From Souk to Souk is based on my experiences and impressions of places I have visited in and around the region. Only Kabul, according to geographers, lies outside it. Often, though, cartographers' borders are somewhat artificial and when I visited Afghanistan it was clear that the cultural influences of the Middle East extend here too. Alexander the Great, whose exploits brought him to various cities featured in this book, founded several towns in what is today Afghanistan. And, given that the country also shares a religious heritage with the Middle East, I could not resist featuring the Afghan capital.

The vast majority of the people I met during my visits were friendly, kind and showed an intense interest in the world beyond the borders of their own country. For many of them, overseas travel is not an option and, when it does occur, sadly it is sometimes as a refugee, fleeing the sectarian unrest and internecine struggles that continue to plague parts of the region. Indeed, some of the cities I visited have, in the meantime, become caught up in the Arab spring, leaving me wondering what has happened to the people I met there. I have deliberately chosen not to write from the perspective of hindsight, choosing instead to describe the people and places as they were when I encountered them. And, it has to be said, most of the people I met were men: in many of the countries, for cultural reasons, social interaction with local women is simply not possible.

Turmoil is not new to the area. In the course of the centuries, the lands of the Middle East have been united under, and divided by, seemingly countless empires and kingdoms; they have been brought together through trade and wrought asunder by warfare. From this perspective, today's frontiers seem to be merely the latest configuration of borders that shift like desert sands. In writing about what are sometimes quite disparate places, I realised that the souks are a common, if variable, element linking these various human settlements not only geographically, but also through time. Some of those that feature in the book have occupied the same sites for centuries, others have evolved to such a degree that they are now souks in little more than name.

From Souk to Souk is not a chronological travelogue. It does not claim to be journalistic reporting, but nor is it pure fiction. Rather, it weaves observations with perceptions and memories with imagination. After all, who, when visiting such a beguiling and exotic collection of lands, could be expected to return with a clear head and untouched by their enchantment?

Robin Ratchford

Journey to the Centre of the World

'Hello, my friend! Where are you from?'

The voice jolted me from my thoughts. I looked up to see a man in his early twenties with an earnest and friendly aspect, on whose thin lips hung a nervous smile. His blue jeans and polo top with its little animal motif on the breast appeared smart enough, but his footwear betrayed his modest background.

'I'm British,' I said, after some hesitation, 'but I live in Belgium.' I was slightly alarmed, but let my face freeze into an expression that I hoped would not show it.

'London?'

'No, Brussels.'

'Ah, *Bruxelles!*' he beamed after a momentary blank expression, apparently delighted at having found a hook for continuing the conversation. 'I have a cousin there. *Vous-parlez français?*' His accent was strong, his effort determined, his regard interesting.

Byzantium, Constantinople, Istanbul: three names for a city that conjures up notions of the exotic as few others do. Fabulous mosques and minarets, sultans in magnificent costumes and outrageous turbans, beautiful and ambitious women behind the closed doors of mystical harems, regimes at once incomprehensible and cruel: these are just some of the archetypal images that through the ages have been associated with the city on the Bosphorus. But the erstwhile capital of so many great empires represents more than anything a grand cultural bazaar where the small continent of Europe ends and the vast and populous landmass that is Asia begins.

It would be in this city that I would spend the last days of the twentieth century: not the simple, chronological hundred years, the passing of which was indicated by a date ending in two zeros and fêted by parties and fireworks, but the century whose end would be marked by an event that represented the opening of a door into a new, different era. In the same way that historians sometimes view the eighteenth century as a concept ending not in 1799 but in 1815 and the nineteenth in 1914 rather than 1899, I doubt future chroniclers will conclude that the twenty-first century began in 2000.

Istanbul was also where I began my travels to the Eastern Mediterranean and the Middle East. It was not my first visit to a Muslim land: I had already been to Morocco, but although it is an Islamic country, both its capital Rabat and the iconic city of Casablanca lie further west than either Barcelona or Madrid and face the chilly, tempestuous Atlantic rather than the sparkling and constant *Mare Nostrum*. It is not merely a question of longitude or tides, of course: Asia Minor and the Middle East are among the cradles of civilisation with many cities in the Fertile Crescent having been inhabited for thousands of years. The trip to Istanbul was my first foray into this beguiling world steeped in history. Like so many before me, and perhaps like you, too, I was tempted by the lure of the Orient and its promise of the exotic, of the unknown, and of seeing with my own eyes that which I knew only from countless tales and fables, history books and films. I was hungry to see what really lay behind the gossamer drapes of Turkishness that hung like so many cultural veils between the Levant and those as yet innocent of its ways. And I was thirsty to drink of its pleasures, to taste the wine of the country on my lips and in my mouth, to recline on its divans and let the aromatic smoke of a thousand *nagilehs* transport me to another world. To the uninitiated, the turbans and harems have been replaced by blood-red fezzes, the dark prisons of *Midnight Express* and perhaps a vague recollection of the mood captured in a happier film, the wonderfully atmospheric *Topkapi*. The reality is, of course, different, but traces of these elements still exist in some form or other: that is what makes the city so exciting.

'Really? You have a cousin in Brussels?' I asked, not overly surprised. 'Yes, there are lots of Turks there. *Mais vous parlez français?*' My eagerness to escape from whatever the young man in front of me wanted to sell or beg for was blunted by my curiosity as to his language skills.

'No, that's all I can say,' he laughed, displaying a mouthful of white but rather uneven teeth as he sat down on the bench next to me. 'You are a tourist?'

'I'm just visiting,' I smiled, unconsciously inching away from him.

'What would you like to see? You have been to Topkapi?'

'No, not yet,' I said, clearing my throat.

As I contemplated the delights of Istanbul from the comfort of my plane seat, it was difficult to determine whether the frisson my imaginings provoked were of excitement, of fear, or a dangerous melange of both. Yet I sensed that, somewhere in my subconscious, there simmered a worry that the experience might not live up to expectations. If I had looked a little deeper, though, I might have realised that the apprehension I felt was about something else altogether.

As the aircraft began its final descent, the unpromising view from the window was of a vast metropolis, home to millions and blanketed by an uninviting brown smog. I landed at Atatürk Airport, so modern that it could have been anywhere in Europe and which, technically speaking, is indeed on the Old Continent. The Istanbul I had come to discover was, of course, also a shining example of a secular Islamic country, a beacon of hope that other states in the region could also develop into modern democracies. The creation of the Turkish Republic after the fall of the Ottoman Empire had seen the introduction of a temporal constitution, the replacement of traditional clothing with Western attire, the adoption of the Latin alphabet and, before Belgium, France or Italy, even votes for women. Turkey, I thought, but above all Istanbul, surely proved that secular Islam was possible and that a clash of civilisations between East and West need not be inevitable.

The adrenalin-rush ride to the hotel in the small yellow taxi felt like one of the more frightening computer games as, tyres squealing, we swerved between cars filled with families or watermelons and raced past growling lorries churning out clouds of black smoke. My moustachioed cabbie blasted out a tune on the horn, impatiently cursing any driver who did not immediately get out of our way, which was most of them. When we finally pulled up outside the hotel in the historical Sultanahmet quarter, I felt myself physically deflate with relief that we had arrived in one piece and had to virtually peel my hand off the grab handle, such was the tightness of my grip.

During the hair-raising journey from the airport my entire attention had been focused on the road and the blur of passing vehicles. Now, as I clambered out of the car, I felt I had been transported to a different world: it was as if the jolting experience of the taxi ride had served to exorcise the memory of the airport's modernity and by a strange motorised catharsis deliver me to a more traditional Turkey. Rising above the trees like a scene from *Tales from the Thousand and One Nights* were the minarets and domed roofs of the Blue Mosque and the Hagia Sophia. Here was the quintessential view of Istanbul, of its exoticism, of its Islamic nature, despite the Turkish state being secular and the 1500-year-old Hagia Sophia no longer a mosque but since 1935 a museum. These iconic buildings announced to me that I had arrived in the Levant even before I had crossed the Bosphorus into Asia Minor. I stared at the two monolithic structures and felt a wave of excitement trickle over my body as I finally accepted that I was in Istanbul, surrounded by its beauty and its history, its temptations and its dangers.

A couple of hours later, I found myself inside the Hagia Sophia. It had beckoned me, absorbed me, and surrounded me. In contrast to many historic sites that one sees, the edifice requires no imagination to visualise how it might have been: like Rome's Pantheon, it stands virtually intact, a would-be portal to antiquity. Originally a Christian church, it was the first basilica to be built with a high dome, setting an architectural trend that lasts to this day, in St Peter's in Rome and in St Paul's in London. Standing below the cupola that had already existed for half a millennium when William the Conqueror first stepped on English soil, I marvelled at its height, equivalent to a twenty-storey building, and wondered how it would have seemed to past generations used only to low – and lowly – dwellings. I wanted to lie on my back on the cold stone floor so I could contemplate the dome's expanse, but I knew it was impossible: this Grande Dame would take instant offence and send her guards scurrying to remove me. And, besides, I dared not.

Christian saints stared down from golden mosaics, their expressions as paralysed as the day Constantinople finally fell to

Ottoman forces led by Sultan Mehmet II, an indecently young 21-year-old when he proudly rode his armies through the gates of the city. On that May day in 1453, under the same hapless gaze of these saints, throngs of Christians sought divine protection behind the bronze gates of the Hagia Sophia, only to be sold into slavery by their captors. Next to these ineffectual symbols of Christendom, sensual Arabic calligraphy with its beautiful – but to me unintelligible – Koranic declarations seemed to float like strange sheet music accessible only to believers. In that great space, I felt small and transient, my presence, my life, but a momentary flash on a timeless scene. I walked in, around and out of the Hagia Sophia like an insignificant extra in a vast oeuvre I did not understand.

Later that day, as I stared at the floodlit views of these magnificent buildings in the gathering dusk, I knew that, atmospheric though it was, the sight before me was something very recent: during the eras of which they are so evocative, after dark these two great structures would have been no more than silhouettes against the starlit skies of ancient times. Now, I could not decide if they were basking in the glory of the floodlights or felt blinded by the glare of a world that left them no peace, even at night.

I was in the *Sultanahmet Meydanı*, the park set out on the site of the huge hippodrome, first built 1800 years ago and expanded under the Roman Emperor Constantine a century later. In Ottoman times, it was the sporting and social focal point of the city. Today, the leisure activities are more low-key and certainly more peaceful, with Turkish families wandering round the grounds or sitting on the slatted benches, chatting and eating roasted chickpeas, sunflower seeds and nuts from small paper cones. I passed old men watching the world go by or playing backgammon. The click-clack of the wooden checkers on the board mixed with the laughter of small children who, clutching foil balloons on sticks, ran around enjoying the open space, no doubt a welcome contrast to the cramped apartments in which I imagined they lived. Spotting an empty seat, I decided to sit down and savour the atmosphere of my first Turkish evening. In front of me, I recognised a Judas tree – so called because Judas Iscariot is said to have hanged himself from one – its bright pink spring flowers a result of it blushing with shame. It was the end of summer, though, and tonight there was no evidence of ignominy, the specimen opposite just a sombre mosaic of dark green and black in the fading light. The squeaks of bats swooping and darting, erratic tiny shadows against the darkening sky, filled the balmy evening air. And, beyond the oasis that was the *Sultanahmet Meydanı*, murmured the constant background noise of this city of millions.

It was as I was reflecting on my first day in Istanbul that this lanky young man had appeared in front of me and started up a conversation I was not looking for.

'*Türkçe konuşuyorsunuz değil mi?*' he asked, looking at the copy of *Hürriyet* in my hand and raising a dark eyebrow with contours so perfect it could have been plucked.

I find carrying a local newspaper can be an effective way of fooling all manner of street vendors and stallholders into thinking one lives locally, with the happy result of being spared many a tiresome sales pitch. Clearly, though, the young man next to me had not been deterred and had pushed his way through my first line of defence with disconcerting ease.

'No, not really. Just a little bit,' I fibbed, standing up. I had only guessed what he had asked and in fact speak no Turkish at all.

'I can show you Istanbul,' he offered, also rising to his feet. 'I am a history student: I know lots about the city. I can show you many interesting things.'

Was that enthusiasm or desperation in his hazel eyes, I wondered?

'Thank you, but I don't need a guide,' I smiled, instantly regretting the words.

'How much do you want to pay?' he persisted, his accent becoming slightly stronger.

'Well, nothing actually. I don't need a guide.' I shrugged and formed my mouth into a sort of helpless smile. Once again, I had painted myself into a corner with my stubbornness. 'Thank you, anyway.'

I turned and began walking away as casually as I could, conscious of the embrace of the warm city air. A moment later, I realised my would-be guide was following me, clearly determined not to give up so easily.

'How much do you want to pay?' he repeated.

The next morning I had breakfast on the rooftop restaurant of my hotel, from which I had a panoramic view across the city, already humming and sparkling with life, a flash of morning sunshine occasionally reflecting off distant panes of glass across the water, perhaps a window opening, a car turning: a banal action in an anonymous life that unknowingly sent a momentary twinkle into my own. I sipped my cappuccino: I was not yet ready for a Turkish coffee.

I pondered on how, considering it was one of the oldest parts of Istanbul, the Sultanahmet quarter was surprisingly open and leafy. Yet, beneath the thin veneer of green lay 25 centuries of history and, from the division of the Roman Empire in AD 395 to the end of the Ottoman Empire in 1922, this city had been the seat of power for over 120 emperors and sultans. As I had walked past the neat lawns and flower beds of the *Sultanahmet Meydanı* the day before, it had been hard to believe that the site of this formal park was once considered the centre of the world, the nearby Million Stone marking the spot from where, after the Emperor Constantine made the city his eponymous capital in AD 330, all roads in the Roman Empire began. Wandering around the site of the former hippodrome, I had realised it was only time, not space, that separated me from the 100,000 spectators who once filled its terraces to watch and bet on the chariot races, the four teams each sponsored by a different political party in the Senate. The crowds that cheered the Blues, the Greens, the Reds and the Whites and, on occasion, rioted on an unimaginable scale, sometimes leaving tens of thousands dead, were no more, their shouts and cries forever lost on the winds of the Bosphorus, the atoms and elements that made up their bodies since reincarnated countless times in all the things we see around us – in ourselves even. I had looked at the palms of my hands and considered whether the carbon, iron and copper within me had previously existed in the body of one of those men or women. Yet what, I had wondered, had happened to their souls? Had they been simply discarded on a current of sea air in the same way as their words and laughter? As the day had drawn to a close and the shadows across the park had grown longer, I had become increasingly aware of the contrast between the longevity of the urban creation around me and the ephemeral existence of those who walked its streets. Now, in the bright light of the morning, yesterday's thoughts seemed almost as distant as the Constantinople of the Eastern Roman Empire.

I finished my coffee, checked my watch and went down to the lobby where I found Osman already waiting for me. He had scrubbed up well and was sporting a perfectly ironed white shirt, together with the same pointy shoes as the evening before. He seemed relieved and greeted me effusively whilst throwing a triumphant glance at the grey-haired receptionist who was watching us from behind the counter.

'I want to take you somewhere special,' he announced. 'Come!' And, lightly touching my arm, he ushered me out on to the street, his sudden physical proximity bringing with it the heady notes of fresh perspiration beneath a vigorous cologne.

'First time in Istanbul?' His tone was an odd mix of the cheerful and the serious.

'Yes,' I nodded.

'Then I will show you everything.'

Over breakfast, my doubts about employing the services of a guide had crept back, but Osman had a certain charm and I could hardly have stood him up. Still too early for the big tourist groups, the streets of Sultanahmet were strangely quiet and after just a few minutes' walk we arrived at a small, single-storey building above which towered a section of some ancient wall, its uneven stones held together with mortar mixed by long-forgotten hands. Leaving the early autumn sunlight behind, I followed Osman through the doorway and descended countless steps into a cool underworld at the entrance of which stood an unassuming ticket office.

'This is the Basilica Cistern,' he smiled. 'In Turkish it is called the *Yerebatan Sarayı*; it means Sunken Palace.' Something in the tone of Osman's voice made me think he was beginning a well-rehearsed spiel.

The Turkish designation captures the splendour of this hidden marvel much more effectively than its English name, which makes it sound like some sort of giant porcelain fitting for a Victorian bathroom. The muted light revealed a vast underground hall with over three hundred Ionic and Corinthian marble columns rising eerily out of water, balanced on motionless mirror images like a setting from some fantasy tale. If one were ever to find the ruins of Atlantis, I thought, surely this is what they would look like. For a moment, I forgot about Osman, my thoughts captivated by the scene around me. I half expected a monstrous serpent to come writhing its way through the silent waters or to see the stalking shadow of some mythical beast on the gently under-lit walls. Instead, in a far corner, I found two carved Medusa heads, one upside down, one on its side, serving as bases for the columns above them. Only the distant drip, drip of water broke the silence in this less well-known of Istanbul's sights, but which, for me, remains to this day one of its most magical.

'In the past, they used it to store water,' whispered Osman, slipping back into my world. 'In the Byzantine period, they built lots of them underneath the city. You see, Istanbul has many hidden attractions,' he smiled.

Back in the daylight of the city above, we made our way towards the Grand Bazaar. By now, shiny coaches with oversized wing-mirrors resembling giant insect antennae had begun disgorging their cargoes of tourists, and Germans, Spaniards and Italians in ill-fitting summer wear were waddling around the Sultanahmet district like flocks of stray geese. As we passed them, I caught snippets of conversations: a remark about Ludwig next door, a comment on breakfast, a question to Maria; momentary glimpses into lives in Bremen, Alicante and Milan.

'First, I want to show you something,' Osman said, bringing me abruptly back from my social eavesdropping. 'You are a Christian, yes?'

'Nominally,' I murmured.

Minutes later, I was standing in front of the fourth-century Constantine Column while Osman took a picture. With this piece of Roman art towering above me, I was unconvinced that the result of my eager guide's photographic efforts would be particularly memorable given that he was standing only a few paces away.

'There is a secret chamber underneath the column containing

the nails used in the crucifixion,' he explained in a matter-of-fact tone as he handed me my camera back, 'and pieces of the cross itself.'

It seemed an improbable tale and sounded as if it had been lifted from the script of an *Indiana Jones* movie, but I decided not to question it, instead politely just making appropriate noises of interest. Although Istanbul today lies in a Muslim country, it does indeed have a long and important history as a Christian city. The adoration of relics, however, whatever their denomination, remains anathema to me. I had read that the Topkapi Palace a mere stone's throw away on the Seraglio Point was crammed with artefacts from Mecca and Medina, but I had little interest in seeing the cabinets full of casts of footprints, cuttings of toenails, and hair from Mohammed the Prophet and the first caliphs.

We continued to the Grand Bazaar, weaving our way past guides waving flags and umbrellas as they endeavoured to herd their shuffling tour groups.

'It was built in the mid-fifteenth century,' proclaimed Osman as we passed through the stone entrance, leaving the Levantine sunshine behind us, 'and then renovated in 1894 after an earthquake. It has more than 3,000 shops and nearly 60 covered streets.' He was lapsing into his spiel again.

My first impressions of the *Kapalicarsi*, or covered bazaar, were completely different to what I had expected. Instead of narrow alleyways, it was, in places, more like an earlier version of a contemporary shopping mall with long, broad passages lined with modern-style stores and covered by a high, arched roof. Turks and tourists alike wandered along, checking out the shop windows. Further in, though, the streets became narrower and glass-fronted shops gave way to open-fronted stalls. Displays of kilims, rugs, spices, silver coffee pots and gaily decorated earthenware bowls poured out on to the tiled floor and fabulous glass lamps, colourful beads, and amulets to ward off the evil eye hung from the walls. Here, the bewildering quantity of objects and the myriad of colours, the twinkling of lights and the sparkling of polished metal, the pungent aromas and the zesty fragrances were an assault on the senses. Who could walk past such a cornucopia and not be enticed to linger, to look, to smell, to touch and finally to end up desiring, needing and buying some fine – or not so fine – object? This was the bazaar as I had imagined it.

'You would like to buy some souvenirs?' It sounded more like a command than a question, yet I also detected a timbre of optimism in Osman's voice.

'No, not really,' I replied: I, for one, could certainly withstand stocking up on the various wares on offer. 'My house is full of stuff already.'

'There are beautiful carpets here,' Osman insisted. 'They would look very nice *chez vous*!'

'I'm sure they are wonderful,' I retorted, hearing my own impatience and ignoring his attempt at French, 'but I have nowhere to put them.' I was determined not to leave the Grand Bazaar laden with tat or, even worse, having signed up to the industrial-scale export of Turkish furnishings back to my home in Belgium. I should have expected that Osman would know at least one of the store keepers and, despite my declarations, our seemingly casual meander through the vast indoor market was clearly choreographed to ensure we ended up at the shop of a carpet seller he knew.

'These carpets are very good quality!' whispered Osman, in what was evidently meant to be a confidential tone, his breath warm on my ear, his hand closing round my arm.

The esteemed purveyor of the rugs in question was a middle-aged man with bulging pug-dog-like eyes and whose clothes stretched over his rotund body like some fitted cover. He tried to wave me into his shop with a greasy grimace, an ingratiating bow and a dramatic sweep of the arm, promising tiny cups of tea without any obligation to buy. I resisted temptation and thanked him with a firm smile before determinedly drifting away. Osman scuttled after me.

'You can look for free,' he pleaded. 'You don't have to buy anything!'

But, this time, what was on offer really did not interest me.

Half an hour later, passing the earthy, red and golden hues of a row of fragrant spice stores, we emerged blinking from the Grand Bazaar and headed towards the Galata Bridge. I was trying not to be annoyed with my guide and kept telling myself that being herded into a carpet shop was all part of the experience. Ferries, their bright bunting fluttering in the breeze, lined the shore at Eminönü as they waited to take people to the Asian side or up the Bosphorus; others sailed back and forth on the sparkling waters, picture-book images in a three-dimensional gallery. As I watched the multi-coloured mass of people swarming along the quay, I forgot the carpet incident, my eyes wandering instead to the bridge in the distance on which minute figures and colourful cars passed the rows of fishermen standing patiently by their rods.

'That is the Galata Tower,' said Osman, waving a slender finger towards the other shore of the Golden Horn, where a round, pointed-top structure of the sort one imagines Rapunzel living in looked decidedly out of place amongst the shabby modern buildings surrounding it. On our side of the water, trams trundled by, flags flapped and seagulls soared and swooped on salty thermals. I paused to watch the vast kaleidoscope of constant movement and colour and tried to imagine how the same scene might have looked five hundred or even a thousand years ago.

Osman suggested we take a boat ride, an idea that had instant appeal and no obvious catches. As our ferry chugged its way along the Bosphorus, the breeze blowing down from the Black Sea provided a cooling respite from the sun. My companion stood sipping the small glass of steaming *çay*, or Turkish tea, handed him by a steward in a rather scruffy burgundy waistcoat and with a greying, walrus moustache. The boat gently rose and fell on the brown waters that linked the Mediterranean with what the ancient Greeks called the Hospitable Sea. I watched as the portly waiter drifted between the passengers, deftly balancing his laden tray. We had been among the last to board the busy *feribot* and so had been too late to find seats. Some, like us, were standing, but many were tightly ensconced on the wooden benches, scarves tied round their heads, bulging shopping bags at their feet. The upper deck with its panoramic view of the passing cityscape had been particularly full, crammed with both locals and tourists, so instead we leant against the railing down below and watched as we glided past the Dolmabahçe and Çirağan Palaces. The Bosphorus seemed to lap at their elegant façades, so low was the land on which they stood and yet, as if mere ghosts from the past, they left no reflection in the turbid liquid before them.

'How many more years do you have left to study?' I asked Osman.

'Two, perhaps three,' he shrugged, watching the foam from the bow churn as the ferry ploughed its way northwards.

'And what do you want to do when you have finished?'

'I'd like to travel, to go to Europe, or America, but it's expensive.'

'Yes, and I suppose you need a visa too,' I reflected.

A young woman in a floral summer dress, her blonde hair blowing in the light breeze, walked up and stood next to us to take some photographs of the view upstream, the expensive-looking camera round her neck firing off a rapid series of clicks. When she had finished, she turned to look at us, blue eyes sparkling quizzically before a friendly smile briefly lit up her freckled face. A moment later she was gone.

15

'Have you already done your military service?' I ventured a few moments later.

Osman nodded, swallowing and pressing his thin lips together; his thoughts seemed elsewhere.

'And where would you like to go in Europe?' I asked.

'To Germany, to London,' he said rather vaguely, rubbing the smooth skin of his chin. And then, turning to face me, he smiled and added after a pause, 'perhaps to see my cousin in *Bruxelles*.'

'What about America? Where would you like to go there?'

'New York.' He sounded more resolute. 'In America you can make big money and everyone is welcome. Here in Turkey it is not easy to find a good job.'

I pondered Osman's claimed area of study, Turkish history, and wondered how easy it would be to find a well-paid position anywhere with that as his qualification. As we sailed under the Bosphorus Bridge, its span high above us cast a momentary, cooling shadow over the boat. We watched the passing scenery slowly mutate from bustling cityscape with its palaces and mosques to more genteel suburbia where generous waterside apartment blocks and mansions were backed by green, forested hills across which the first shades of autumn were starting to appear. To our left lay Europe, to the right, Asia.

'Do you like it?' asked Osman, pointing to the view with his free hand.

'Yes, I do,' I smiled. 'It's very pretty.'

'I'm sure you will like Anadolu Kavagi. Not many tourists go there, mostly just Turkish people. There are lots of good restaurants where you can eat fish.' His English was good, but sometimes he sounded as if he were reciting sentences from a phrase book.

I began to suspect a proposal of lunch was looming as a way of Osman getting a free meal. The memory of the carpet shop incident slunk back and hissed that I should be irked at the prospect of feeding him, but I felt it would be churlish to wriggle out of what was for me a small outlay, whereas for the young student it might be the only square meal he would get that day.

As we passed under the second great bridge, the *Fatih Sultan Mehmet Köprüsü*, I saw something dark curve out of the water ahead before slipping back under the gentle waves. I strained my eyes; there it was again, and then again. To my surprise, dolphins were swimming here in the Bosphorus, one of the world's busiest shipping lanes.

'Look, Osman!' I cried.

'Yes,' he smiled, seemingly unfazed by the sighting. 'You often see them here.' Then, registering my excitement, he added enthusiastically, 'You see, I told you I would show you lots of interesting things!'

He finished his *çay*, placing the little glass on the waiter's tray as the latter did his rounds to collect the empties, and then pulled out a packet of cigarettes, which he waved in my direction. I smiled and shook my head.

Eventually, after several stops along the way, the *feribot* pulled into its last port of call, Anadolu Kavagi, a small fishing village on the Asian side just before the entrance to the Black Sea. Here, the houses seemed to dip their toes in the rippling waters of the Bosphorus. Stacked next to each other like tightly-packed coloured boxes, many were just one room wide, yet most had a balcony on each of their three or four storeys. A flotilla of small boats was moored in front of the village, the hues of their painted woodwork reflected in a shimmering palette on the water. I walked across the short gangplank and took my first steps onto Asian soil, a strange sensation and something of an anticlimax: no elephants, no pagodas, no rice paddies, just this small settlement at the water's edge. The centre of the village had been taken over by a cluster of touristic restaurants which, from the look of the customers at the plastic tables, catered mainly to the domestic market, just as Osman had said. A small girl saw me looking and stared back with big brown eyes, a French fry on her fork suspended momentarily in front of two rows of teeth before disappearing into the closing gap between them. The overall effect was not quite as picturesque as I had envisaged, but I imagined Osman's mouth already watering at the prospect of lunch. I was sure I saw the nostrils at the end of his long nose twitching as a cocktail of smells, predominantly fish, garlic and cooking fat, drifted towards us from the row of eateries where Turkish families seated under tilting parasols were tucking into plates of food with gusto. We walked around for a few minutes, avoiding the few shops selling garish toys and cheap souvenirs, but there was not much to see or do except have lunch and the *feribot* was not due to return to Istanbul for another three hours. Osman, it seemed, had organised our journey to the other continent perfectly.

A while later, we had finished our grilled fish, which was better than I expected, and were taking it in turns to suck on a large *nagileh*, the fragrant double apple smoke hanging expectantly in the air as the early autumn sun warmed our faces. My guide for the day had insisted that the *shisha* was all part of my Istanbul experience and so, emboldened by two large *Efes* Pils, I had given in to persuasion. Now, I could feel myself starting to get high on the tobacco, a heady mix with the alcohol. Osman, who had also downed a couple of beers and had clearly enjoyed his meal, took one more drag on the *shisha* pipe before offering it back to me. Was it really so addictive, I thought as I puffed away, or was my enthusiasm purely psychological?

'Would you like to see the castle?' asked Osman, the last of the *shisha* smoke drifting out of his mouth as casually as the question.

'What?' I spluttered, coughing on the aromatic veil that was enveloping my face. 'What castle?'

'Yoros Castle,' he replied, with an indifferent nod suggesting it lay somewhere behind the restaurant.

'Why didn't you say so before?' The words flew forth in something between a squeak and a growl. My irritation was clear because I already knew the answer to the question: lunch.

The castle ruins were perched on a hill above the village. How I had not spotted them from the ferry remains a mystery. It was a steep walk up the wooded rise, one that would have been done more easily on an empty stomach, but we were at the top sooner than I expected and, if I am honest, the exercise helped digest the rather oily meal. The grassy area in front of the castle was not very crowded: a couple of families meandered about while some teenage lads sat on the stone walls, chatting and laughing. There was not much of the fort left: the most impressive part was the two towers of what had once been the main gate.

'There is a good view from the other side,' said Osman.

We picked our way through the ruins to emerge onto a spectacular vista where the Bosphorus met the Black Sea. As I gazed northwards, I realised that Istanbul was not only a bridge connecting east and west, but also a link between north and south, with Ukraine and Russia somewhere over the horizon. For them, the Bosphorus was the gateway to a different world, to the Sea of Marmara and the Mediterranean, and to North Africa beyond. And when the Vikings came from Sweden to the city they called *Miklagård,* it was along the rivers of the Slavic lands and across the Black Sea that they sailed. I began to understand why Istanbul was once considered the centre of the world. And I realised that the city represented for me, too, the passage from a familiar universe to a new one and a doorway to the Orient.

Almost imperceptibly, as if drawn by some irresistible force, distant ships were making their way across the still water towards the mouth of the world's narrowest strait open to international shipping. There are those who worry that one day an oil tanker might have an accident, its fuel leaking or exploding with disastrous consequences for the vulnerable city that hugs the shores of the Bosphorus. Looking southwards to this cleavage between Europe and Asia, I wondered if the ancient Greeks who had first settled Byzantium and the southern littoral of the Black Sea had once imagined their gods wrenching the two continents apart in some mythical battle. A shadow crossed the waters below, its bird-like shape changing as it passed over the hill on the other side. Looking up, I saw a plane, the whistling of its engines only now becoming audible as it gradually descended towards the airport in the distance.

'You like the view?'

Once again, I had momentarily forgotten my young Turk.

It was late afternoon when our ferry docked back at Eminönü, thick smoke billowing from its funnel into the clear autumn sky as it slowly came alongside the quay. I had thought our day would finish after the boat trip and that we would now say our farewells, so I was surprised by Osman's next proposal.

'Now I will show you another part of Istanbul,' he said, as we disembarked surrounded by jostling crowds of commuters, day-trippers and shoppers, all eager to push their way off first.

I followed Osman over the busy Galata Bridge, but when we reached the other side, instead of heading towards the fairytale tower, he veered to the right where we began the ascent of a steep, narrow street. Small, scruffy shops piled high with stereo equipment and car radios were interspersed with others selling guitars, drums and traditional musical instruments. Outside some of the hi-fi shops, youths in tight-fitting T-shirts and cheap jeans chatted with the owners. Business in violins and tambourines was even slower.

The wizened men in shabby grey suits from another era sat on stools in front of their shops watching silently as we wended our way up the hill, occasionally blowing a cloud of smoke from their cigarettes. Eventually, we reached the top and the glorified alley opened out into a sort of small square.

'This is the start of the main shopping street in Istanbul,' said Osman, '*İstiklâl Caddesi*.'

Ahead of me was an unimpressive pedestrianised road with few shops and not many punters. Looks were deceiving, though, and as we walked along we passed the Swedish Consulate, a veritable palace behind iron gates and the country's embassy when the city was still the capital of the Ottoman Empire. A little further on, we paused to look at the Russian and Dutch counterparts, which had similar histories and were equally impressive. Gradually, the street became wider and busier and the shops more interesting, selling everything from clothes to CDs, kitchenware to sports goods. We walked past buildings in an eclectic mix of styles: neo-classical, neo-gothic, renaissance revival and even art deco. The medley of nineteenth- and twentieth-century architecture lent Independence Avenue, to give it its English name, a distinctly cosmopolitan air.

'This is the Galatasaray school,' announced Osman, stopping in front of a large, nineteenth-century building incongruously painted in Habsburg yellow. 'It is one of the best schools in Turkey: the pupils study in Turkish and French. And here is also where the football team started.'

I smiled to myself: Osman's presentation sounded as if he had learnt it from a script, but I had to admire the effort he was making. My thoughts drifted back to the crowd violence of the ancient hippodrome, a tradition that Turkish football supporters, including those of Galatasaray, seemed keen to continue, albeit on a smaller scale. Here was I, centuries later, in a city vastly different in so many ways from the Constantinople of old and yet some aspects continued as a part of the cultural fabric. Superficially, the event may have evolved, but I knew that the continuity between the chariot races of the past and the football matches of today found its basis in human nature, in emotions and tribalism. These were the lifeblood that fuelled the elation, the cheering, the anger, the violence.

The early evening was clearly the time Turks like to go out shopping or simply meander arm in arm, talking and checking out those around them. By the time we reached the main retail stretch of *İstiklâl Caddesi* it was thronging with people – young people. In Europe, I was used to seeing grey-haired masses shuffling around in beige anoraks, so it was striking to be somewhere where the population was overwhelmingly youthful. It was bustling, it was lively: it felt like the future. Amid the Turkish pop music blaring out of some of the shops I recognised the voice of Tarkan singing *Sımarık*, the 'Kiss Kiss' song, while, high above, swallows screeched as they arched and swooped in the polluted evening sky. Headscarves and long dresses mingled with miniskirts and revealing necklines; loosely draped robes and shapeless suits contrasted with tops and trousers that stretched seductively over well-formed bodies, but, despite the great contrasts, the overwhelming impression was of Westernness. Chain stores that could be found on most European high streets alternated with Turkish shops selling domestic versions of the same. It was as if all Istanbul were packed into the three-kilometre length of *İstiklâl Caddesi*. Apart from the fact that everyone was so young, this busy thoroughfare could have been anywhere in Europe. I realised that the historic Sultanahmet district with its throngs of tourists was as typical of Istanbul as the Grand-Place was of Brussels.

Startled by the sound of an engine, I turned round to see two black motorbikes revving their way slowly through the crowd that parted deferentially to let them pass. Each bike had a driver and pillion passenger, both in black and red leathers, eyes and thoughts concealed behind dark glasses. As they drove slowly in front of us, one of the pillions turned to look at me, but in her mirrored lenses I saw only my own reflection.

'That is *Yunus polisi*, the Dolphin Police,' said my young guide, with what I thought was a touch of pride.

The crowd closed behind the two bikes and soon they were out of sight, the noise of their engines no longer audible.

'You look tired,' said Osman. 'Would you like to try a Turkish coffee? I know a nice place near here where we can go.'

'That sounds like a good idea,' I agreed. I was indeed starting to flag.

'Would you like to try some Turkish delight as well?' he smiled.

Like so many fast-developing cities, Istanbul seems eager to shed many of the aspects of its history that the visitor finds most appealing. In a flush of *arrivisme*, it seeks to demolish that which has character and replace it with modern blandness, which in a few years will be decrepit and dated. Out with the bathwater of underdevelopment goes the baby of heritage and culture. In this sprawling metropolis one sees a bewildering mix of old and new, rich and poor, urban and rural, land and water, fast cars and slow handcarts, pouting lips and shrivelled hands, carved woodwork and sparkling steel. Today, the steel that glistens is on office blocks and designer shopping malls, but in the past it was the flash of swords in battle that caught the sun. Nonetheless, the city has been the site not only of centuries of conflict between Christianity and Islam, but sometimes also of peaceful coexistence between Muslims, Christians and Jews: indeed, after conquering Constantinople, Mehmet II ordered that people from all three Abrahamic faiths across Ottoman lands be resettled in his new capital.

My first visit to Turkey gave me an initial, addictive taste of the Orient and its exotic pleasures, and a desire to explore the rest of the region. In the course of a few days, it showed me a city and a country striving – and in many ways succeeding – to be modern, to be a temporal fulcrum between East and West. Looking out of the window as my plane lifted itself off Turkish soil, I was confident I had seen proof that secular Islam could work, that talk of a clash of civilisations was exaggerated. Yet, only hours later, on a third continent, other airliners flew into the World Trade Center and the Pentagon, shaking that confidence and marking the real and bloody start of a new century. Suddenly, in the time it takes to watch a film, the perceived centre of the world seemed to shift. No doubt like you, as I saw those now famous images, I knew that I was witnessing a pivotal moment in history. Watching events unfold on television at home in *Bruxelles*, I wondered what Osman was making of it all and what the future would now bring for him.

Saul

We heave the rough wooden crate into the back of the car as a plane, rising into the grey Belgian sky, roars overhead. I had not expected the box to be so big, nor for a moment imagined that it would arrive by air, given its weight. The two grumpy customs officials in the dusty, poorly lit office just outside Brussels Airport had been busy making sandwiches with white sliced bread and processed ham. After ignoring me for a couple of minutes, the woman, in her fifties with a thick band of grey roots at the base of her russet hair, had ambled across to the counter. Putting on the glasses that hung round her neck, she had peered suspiciously at the notice I had received telling me where to pick up my delivery. She had removed her spectacles and looked me up and down, her eyes narrowing, before asking me how much the consignment was worth. She had addressed me in French with a thick Flemish accent and so, diplomatically, I had replied in her native tongue. Her lanky, unshaven colleague, some twenty years her junior, had watched on, hunched over his desk, silently munching on his sandwich, until she had told him to go and get the register. Eventually, after some cajoling and apologies for interrupting their meal, I had managed to get the glum duo to hand over the crate without further to-do or, more importantly, payment.

Back at my house, Anton and I carefully set the delivery down in the main corridor. Knowing I would not be able to manage on my own, I had volunteered my Austrian friend to help me in exchange for the promise of a roast-duck dinner served with a bottle of best

Zweigelt, an offer he had eagerly accepted. The crate, covered in red and white 'FRAGILE!' stickers and, somewhat strangely, stamped with half a dozen Chinese characters, is big enough to transport a small child: is my memory playing tricks with me or are the contents larger than I remembered? I fetch a crowbar and begin prising off the lid, while Anton stands watching, arms folded. It sits fast, only coming free with groans of protest as the long nails are wrenched from the coarse timber. When I finally open the crate, I half expect the wisp of some spirit to rise out of it as if an ancient tomb were being exposed. I bend over and part the straw: there it is, staring up at me. To be honest, I am rather surprised it has arrived at all.

'It's wonderful!' said one friend, swigging on her champagne. 'You'll love it, darling, and you simply must go to Palmyra! Agatha Christie stayed there, you know. It's fabulous!' She emptied her glass and looked round expectantly.

'You could spend a whole week just walking round the souk in Damascus!' declared a German friend who had travelled widely in the region.

An entire week? That I doubted, though the message was clear, as was the Teutonic penchant for thoroughness.

'But aren't there secret police following you all the time?' I ventured: after all, under Bashar al-Assad Syria had been branded as being in the Axis of Evil and, as a British citizen, I was concerned that a solo tourist might attract particular attention. Indeed, I wondered whether I might get a hostile reception from people generally were they to discover my nationality.

'Perhaps,' shrugged a third, a Belgian diplomat who had lived and worked in the Syrian capital for three years, 'but I doubt it. It's a really nice place: you should go. You won't regret it.'

Yet again, the taxi driver stopped to ask the way and, once more, the instructions given by a passer-by seemed complicated and involved much gesticulation. The man at the wheel was not put off by the lack of a common language between us and cheerfully reassured me in Arabic that at last he knew where the hotel was. At least I think that is what he said as he babbled on gutturally whilst glancing at me in the rear view mirror, waving a giant hairy hand for emphasis, half its pinkie missing. For a second time, our battered taxi took a large roundabout as we went back on our tracks, the autumn air blowing in my face a welcome respite from the smell of stale tobacco that seemed to have impregnated every molecule of the car. The traffic did not appear to follow any particular rules, vehicles swerving randomly like dodgem cars. Snatches of Arabic disco hits and traditional music mingled with the noise of car horns and racing engines as more adventurous drivers sped past us. Suddenly, we slowed down and veered sharply into a road that led into the old city centre. The rough-shaven cabbie made some announcement while we trundled along a street flanked by shabby market stalls, passing crates of white chickens, boxes of battered vegetables and the occasional sad-looking donkey: I began to wonder about my choice of hotel. A group of schoolgirls in smart uniforms offered a glimmer of hope that civilisation might be just round the corner, but each successive street we entered was narrower than the last and the driver found it increasingly difficult to negotiate his way past the parked vehicles, old bicycles propped against walls and stacks of empty cardboard boxes. Finally, we halted in front of an incongruously smart wooden door in an otherwise nondescript, windowless wall. We were in an impoverished street that did little to instil confidence or a feeling of security. Overhead, generations of twisted wires hung between buildings on either side of the road.

I began to wonder how on earth I would find my way safely from the hotel to any sights of interest.

The driver climbed out of the cab and rang the doorbell with a thick finger. After a few seconds, the door swung open and a smartly-dressed man in a navy blue suit stepped out, his sartorial elegance in abject contrast to the taxi driver's stained T-shirt and fading jeans.

Moments later, I was perched on a velvet sofa, sipping freshly squeezed orange juice. My eyes wandered to the oriental trinkets dangling from the corners of the honey-coloured walls and on to a recent oil painting of old Damascus granted pride of place behind the long wooden reception desk. In just a few paces I had been transported to another world.

'First time in Syria?' asked the receptionist, as he photocopied my passport. When he had welcomed me in front of the hotel, he had introduced himself as Mohammed and, somewhat disconcertingly, had seemed to know who I was before I had even told him my name: were there so few guests, I wondered, or were my fears of surveillance being borne out?

'Yes,' I replied cautiously, placing my empty glass on the octagonal table in front of me.

'Damascus is a nice city, a very old city,' he smiled, ebony eyes studying me as he handed me back my passport. 'I am sure you will enjoy your stay. If you are ready, I will show you to your room.'

Set in the old Jewish quarter, the hotel had once been a private palace. It had been meticulously restored and decorated in traditional Arab style. Mohammed led me down into a large courtyard in which half a dozen empty sun loungers were arranged around a turquoise swimming pool where once the customary central water basin would have been. We crossed the patio, the striped grey and cream lower walls bringing to mind the cathedral in Cordoba, itself once a mosque; above, the plaster was painted a deep, dusky pink. Citrus trees and herbs in terracotta pots lined the walls, their delicate fragrances reminding me of my own patio garden, and thickets of white and pink bougainvillea nestled in the corners. I wondered if the neighbours had any idea of what lay behind the hotel's bland outer walls. As we entered a second, smaller courtyard with a bubbling fountain, Mohammed pulled a large old-fashioned key from his pocket and unlocked one of the three doors that gave on to the patio. My room, reached by going up a couple of steps, was nothing if not opulent, and with its swirling drapes, satin cushions and huge glass chandelier, it looked like a film set. It was very different from the police state I had imagined.

The next day, as the anonymous door of the hotel clicked shut behind me, I felt like I had fallen out of the wardrobe, leaving Narnia behind. Once again, I was in the run-down reality of central Damascus. Only the bright morning sunlight offered any consolation. I followed my instinct and the rather vague map in my guidebook. After a few turns, I found myself in a broad street where vegetable shops, food stores, tiny travel agencies and old houses were lined up one after the other in a jumble of dangerously dilapidated buildings. At the stand nearest to me, a sturdy woman in a brown *abaya* – the traditional loose over-garment worn by women – was unenthusiastically examining the greengroceries: potatoes, root vegetables, courgettes, aubergines and piles of herbs, the last wilting, exhausted. It was not a promising start and yet, according to my map, I was only a stone's throw away from one of the main roads of the Old City. As I passed a barber's shop, a whiff of cheap lemon scent drifted out to greet me. From a slightly fading poster in the window, President Assad looked benevolently over the thin towels hanging on a rickety clothes horse on the street in front. A small boy in oversized *Crocs* and dusty trousers was trying to catch an emaciated kitten, but, skulking nervously below the towels, it kept skipping out of reach every time he got near. In the tiny, brightly lit shop, the grey-haired owner sat reading a newspaper, ignoring the antics outside.

The map proved correct and a few minutes later I found myself on Straight Street and in a distinctly smarter and much renovated environment. The ancient thoroughfare was true to its name and extended into the distance in both directions. Originally laid out by the Greeks and later colonnaded by the Romans for whom it was the *Decumanus Maximus*, it is still the main east-west axis through the old walled city. Today, however, there were no marching legions on what is now known in Arabic as the *Share'a Bab Sharqi*: in fact, it was surprisingly quiet, perhaps because it was still quite early. I headed towards the centre of the old town, its souks and the famous Umayyad mosque. With cars parked along much of its length, the paved one-way street was only wide enough for single-lane traffic. The bay windows of the smart two-storey buildings could easily have been in Spain, while stylish wooden shutters were fastened back on both sides of the open shop fronts exposing an eclectic range of goods. Spangly T-shirts and designer jeans in one store contrasted with traditional Arab dress in the next, and bilious sweets in a tiny outlet presented a kaleidoscope of colour compared to the monochrome display of tin pans just a few paces away.

'Come here, my friend!' called a slim young man from one of several little shops selling dried fruits and nuts. He waved a tanned arm at me and flashed a broad grin. 'Come and try!'

'Thank you,' I smiled back, shaking my head.

'Where are you from?' I heard him call. Perhaps rather unsociably, I did not answer and instead just threw him another smile.

A few minutes later, the street widened out, but was filled with even more parked cars, the latest models of Mercedes standing next to dented Peugeots from a bygone age, shining black metal alongside dust-covered burgundy paintwork. Just beyond the makeshift car park, a crooked house, its two first-floor windows startled eyes, looked as if it was about to collapse. Only the network of cables linking it to its neighbours seemed to hold it in place.

A little further on was the entrance to the Medhat Pasha Souk covering the western end of Straight Street, the shade provided by its high, arched roof a welcome relief. Beams of light dropped in from the small windows along its length, while the numerous holes that pockmarked it shone like tiny stars. A confusing mix of smells danced around me: out of sacks of tea and coffee in one store rose rich and spicy aromas, while the fragrance of lavender, honey and jasmine floated across from neatly stacked little bricks of traditional soap in another. As I sauntered past, I let my eyes wander from shop to shop, from road to roof, from one passer-by to the next.

About halfway through the souk, sunlight flooded in through a gap in the long wall where a street led off, specks of dust floating gently in the haze before me. I turned the opposite direction into the spice souk, its shadowy world lit only by thin shafts of light from little windows high above. The air was buzzing with chatter and market traders' cries and suffused with a cocktail of aromas, the sweet scents of patchouli and sandalwood swirling past the pungent odour of sweat. Trying not to bump into the piles of boxes of mysterious foodstuffs stacked in the middle, I watched the people of Damascus go about their business: scrawny men pushing laden handcarts, stout women in black *abayas*, young ladies in tight jeans and colourful headscarves, lean children in Western clothes, and, among them all, the occasional, self-conscious, sandal-wearing French tourist. Sensing that my curiosity was perhaps verging on the rude, I diverted my eyes to the colourful array of goods piled high in the small shops on each side of the souk: neat rows of boxes, jars, bottles and packets with unintelligible labels lined the shelves while, outside, carefully crafted pyramids of spices in earthy colours rose from large square tins. They looked like the powder paints we used to have at school, but the evocative scents of cinnamon, cardamom and cloves brought incongruous thoughts of Christmas cakes and *Glühwein*, an association reinforced by the ubiquitous cardboard boxes of dates and strings of dried figs. In another shop, a panoply of yarns added to the unusual mixture of goods, the vivid skeins arranged according to colour. A little further on, looking at the delicate domes of dried lavender, saffron and miniature roses that crowned bulging white sacks, I wondered if they really filled the entire bag or just the last quarter, sitting on a sea of polystyrene peanuts or some other more mundane and less expensive material. Gently, I picked up a handful of dried roses, the tiny flowers weighing next to nothing and still fragrant. I suddenly recalled having tried as a young child to make perfume from rose petals in jam jars filled with water: an early and unsuccessful attempt to go into business, the brownish liquid soon smelling only of rotting flowers. And, at that moment, a flurry of other childhood memories came flooding back, here in a world utterly alien to the one in which they were formed.

'Make very nice gift!' said the storekeeper, emerging from his small shop and unknowingly chasing away the ghosts of my past. A carefully trimmed moustache rested on a face that had spent many years in the sun, but his close-set eyes still had a youthful glint to them. 'How much would you like?' Before I had time to think, he produced a brown paper bag and, taking a small aluminium scoop, began filling it.

'How much is it?'

'Is not expensive, my friend,' he smiled, exposing more gaps than teeth. The bag was already brimming with roses. He folded it closed and Sellotaped the flap. 'Four hundred,' he said, holding out the package.

A fait accompli, but a fair price, I thought, handing over my crumpled Syrian pounds. I knew they would make an ideal gift as pot-pourri for a friend, even if in Syria they are often used for culinary purposes. As I returned my wallet to my trouser pocket, instinct made its presence felt and whispered to me that I was being watched. I looked up to see a clean-shaven man in jeans and a navy polo top standing in front of a shop a short distance away, dark eyes observing me. He was partially silhouetted against the daylight at the entrance of the souk, but I felt he had a familiar air. He turned and, picking up something from the display of goods, began talking to the bearded shopkeeper approaching him. I tried to remember if I had seen him elsewhere since arriving in the country: terrible at recalling names, I rarely forget a face, yet I could not bring to mind why this one appeared so familiar.

Continuing in the direction of the Great Mosque that lay just beyond the souk, I paused to look at the items on show outside a couple of traditional pharmacies. Many would not have looked out of place in a Chinese medicine shop: fox pelts and snake skins, dried puffer fish and rabbits' feet dangled above pumice stones and loofahs. I tried to convince myself that some of the more exotic articles were only for decoration and not evidence of a thriving trade in rare animal parts. At a flapping of wings I looked up to see a couple of pigeons vying for space on the sills of one of the windows that ran along the first floor of the long buildings either side of the souk. The rooms behind the dusty panes seemed abandoned and lifeless: the centre of this ancient city was at once busy and bustling, yet so many of the buildings were run-down and empty.

Just beyond the end of the spice souk was the outer wall of the famous eighth-century Great Mosque, built when Damascus was the capital of the Umayyad Caliphate, at the time the largest empire the world had seen, stretching all the way from Portugal to Transoxiana in Central Asia. At the centre of the Old City, it is a powerful symbol of the layers of human history here and the importance of Damascus over the last four thousand years. Today, Syria's pivotal position in the Middle East makes its capital once more a focus of attention, sadly for all the wrong reasons, but it no longer enjoys the commercial or cultural status it once did. I turned and followed the crowd along the lane, the high wall of the mosque towering above me like the bulwark of some forbidden palace. The street soon opened out into a large space in front of the main entrance of the mosque where sellers of Korans, sweets and souvenirs mingled with shoppers, tourists and police. I stopped to look at the Great Mosque, its solid wall of light beige stone contrasting with the peaceful azure sky above. Here, in front of me, stood the fourth-holiest place in Islam, built on top of a Christian basilica reputed to have housed the head of John the Baptist, the relic now having its own shrine within the mosque. The basilica was itself constructed over the largest Roman temple in Syria, dedicated to the god of thunder, Jupiter. This, in turn, had been erected on the site of a temple devoted to the Aramaean cult god of thunderstorms and rain, Hadad, referred to in the Bible as Rimmon. It was the Aramaeans who, entering the city in the eleventh century BC, first made Dimashqu, as they called it, into an important trading centre. And it was their language, Aramaic, that Jesus spoke.

I walked over to the ticket office at the side of the mosque, a few paces from where the tomb of Saladin stood. Nemesis of the Crusaders whom he drove from the Holy Land in the twelfth century, the man had been laid to rest in the city where he had died. I bought a ticket and then walked over to the mosque entrance specially reserved for tourists, where, having taken off my shoes and placed them on the racks with all the others, I entered the main courtyard. It felt strange walking across the smooth floor, my stockinged feet making no sound on the polished limestone, uneven with age. A couple of small groups of Westerners, the women looking rather like monks in the grey, hooded cloaks provided by the mosque authorities, listened to their guides slowly and deliberately explaining the history and features of the elegant building. A few locals wandered around, some taking photographs, others sitting on the warm floor and engaging in small-talk or simply relaxing in the sunshine. The clean lines of the arches and the plain roof somehow managed to blend perfectly with the more ornate architectural elements – Corinthian columns, ceramic tiling and beautiful eighth-century mosaics. The vast courtyard with its long arcades was a haven of calm compared to the bustle of the city outside. In the main prayer hall, I stopped to look at the elaborate marble shrine said to contain the head once delivered on a plate to Salome, the reliquary's green dome giving it the aspect of a gaudy miniature cathedral.

Like so many places in the region, in Damascus historic facts are interwoven with tales born of belief. As I strolled around the mosque, I reflected on how John the Baptist probably did exist, but no-one knew if the head alleged to be in the shrine was really his. According to the New Testament, the saints Paul and Thomas both lived in this city. Paul, formerly Saul of Tarsus, was a Pharisee who zealously persecuted Christians. It was on the road from Jerusalem to Damascus that Jesus is said to have appeared to him in a blinding vision. The New Testament was written in Koine Greek, a dialect then the lingua franca of much of the Mediterranean and the Middle East. The vagaries of Koine vocabulary and grammar mean the description of what happened to Saul that day is open to interpretation when translated: it is not clear if he heard a voice or just a sound, or whether his travelling companions could not hear what he heard or simply could not understand it. The implications for what Saul actually experienced are intriguing: did he really have an encounter with the resurrected Christ, or did he merely suffer from sunstroke or a seizure, the latter causing his temporary blindness? It was not until three days later that Ananias, a disciple of Jesus living in Damascus and following instructions supposedly received from his Lord in a vision, found Saul in a house on the 'Street called Straight' and apparently cured him of his blindness. Once healed, however, Saul saw the light, as it were, converted to Christianity and became the Apostle Paul. One may question the origin or authenticity of Paul's experience, but that he existed as a person does not seem to be in doubt. The city's Jews were angered by his Damascene conversion and he was forced to make a hasty escape in a basket lowered from a window in the city wall. Yet, before taking flight, Paul would have walked along Straight Street, just as I had done earlier that day. Fellow saint, Thomas, even gave his name to one of the city gates and a Christian neighbourhood of old Damascus, Bab Tuma. As I stood in the mosque contemplating the fluid border between fact and belief, I considered how the finer points of linguistics could affect both and, with them, history.

Back outside in the cobbled plaza in front of the mosque, looking at the people, residents of this ancient city as well as visitors, milling around and going about their business, it was strange to think that the scene before me was probably not so different from the one that would have been played out here time and time again over the centuries. In the time of Paul and Thomas, the Temple of Jupiter would have been the main place of Roman worship. Today, the impressive ruins of its western gate with its high arches and the remaining corner of the pediment supported by three towering columns stand between the Great Mosque and the entrance of the Al-Hamidiyah Souk, a reminder of the ephemeral nature of even the greatest empires.

Turning to go into the bazaar, I caught my breath as I thought I recognised the man from the spice souk. A moment later, the figure had melted into the crowd. I wondered if I really was being followed, or if it was just my subconscious playing tricks on me. Certainly, there was no reason for me to arouse anyone's suspicion. Slowly making my way up the broad paved steps towards the souk, I could feel my pulse quickening. I paused at one of the stands selling Korans and, as casually as I could, looked back towards the mosque, half expecting to see cold, dark eyes staring at me, but instead there was just a melee of shoppers and a couple of pale, silver-haired tourists studying an open guide book. Even so, a feeling of unease had begun to ferment in my stomach.

Continuing into the souk, I was surprised to find myself in a seemingly endless nineteenth-century arcade which, with its two-storey colonnaded walls, rows of rectangular windows and arched cast-iron roof, would not have looked out of place in Europe. Like the other souks, rays of daylight fell through windows in the roof high above. The structure itself could have been in Paris, but the brightly lit shops were filled with an assortment of traditional Arab wear ranging from the ubiquitous sombre black *abayas* to glitzy sequined dresses in the gaudiest of colours that could have been lifted from a bad operetta about Marie-Antoinette. Yet it was the number of shop windows openly displaying skimpy and erotic women's underwear that was surprising: Damascus, it seemed, was the lingerie capital of the Middle East.

'You want water, mister?'

I turned to see a young boy in an embroidered waistcoat, baggy trousers and a scarlet fez that had seen better days. On his back hung a large brass samovar almost as big as he was. With rough fingers, he pulled a plastic cup from a stack that was attached to his belt, along with a row of little brass tumblers.

'You want water?' he repeated. A moustache was trying hard to form above his open lips. He looked at me hopefully with grey eyes, but I think he saw the answer already in mine. I sensed that he asked again, this time silently, but the most I was willing to give was a smile. He drifted away, his dishevelled black slippers making no noise on the paving stones.

A little further on, I saw a small crowd gathered outside a wooden-fronted shop selling ice cream. I strained my neck to watch as the staff, in white T-shirts and side caps and wearing surgical gloves, pushed handfuls of the sticky, elastic mixture into cornets. They then rolled them in chopped pistachio nuts before handing them to the waiting clients, who began eagerly devouring their oversized ices. In the background, as if engaged in some tribal ritual, a row of men was rhythmically thrusting long wooden pestles into open-topped churns set into the counter and filled with the coveted white mixture. The *clack-clack* noise of wood on metal sounded like strange experimental music. Above the door, the sign indicated it was the Bakdash ice cream parlour, famous for its *Booza*, a frozen dessert made by pounding a mixture of mastic and sahlab, a flour made from orchid tubers. When my turn came, I pointed to the stack of cornets and moments later took possession of a weighty delight, handed to me by a man with a pointed nose and painter's-brush moustache.

I moved away from the crowd pressing at the counter and looked around at the shoppers, some sauntering, others rushing. Then, a short distance away, I spotted him trying to attract the attention of passers-by. Feeling like a salmon swimming upstream, I made my way through the throng of people, protectively clutching the ice cream close to my chest. When I reached the young water seller, I held out the short cornet with its nut-covered snowball. He looked surprised and reached for a plastic goblet.

'*La*,' I said, 'no water. It's for you.'

For an instant, he looked at me and the ice cream suspiciously before gingerly reaching for it and, after a brief inspection, taking a large, hungry bite. He seemed surprised it was cold and for a moment I thought he was going to spit it out right in front of me, but a second later he began wolfing it down.

I smiled goodbye and continued to amble through the gallery, feeling I was the only person there without an ice cream. The shops were uninspiring, but the ever-growing number of people more than compensated in terms of visual interest. Men, mostly in Western clothes, bustled past, while women in more conservative and distinctly Arabic dress shuffled along, often laden with shopping bags and followed by gaggles of children. Many faces had film-star looks, but others seemed to have been doled out startling combinations of features – elongated faces, horse-like teeth, and bulging eyes – as if the least desirable genes from past invasions had by some misfortune all come together at once. As in most high streets, the multitude was a mix of shoppers and people just walking around, looking, talking, and laughing with their friends and family. The scene was at once familiar and exotic; the ambience was relaxed, yet my thoughts kept returning to the man I suspected was following me. I had done nothing untoward, but perhaps my worst fears were being confirmed.

After a while, I began to bore of the endless shops selling clothes I would never buy and decided to head back. I turned and retraced my steps past the Great Mosque and through to the spice souk, keeping a discreet eye out among the myriad faces for the dark eyes I had seen earlier. In the shadows of the covered market, I began to feel people were observing me: curious glances from shopkeepers, enquiring looks from passers-by, the occasional stare and furtive whisper. Was I imagining it, or were people deliberately bumping into me as I tried to fight my way through the crowds? Out of the corner of my eye, I saw a movement in one of the murky first-floor rooms, a figure slipping out of view behind the dusty glass as I looked up. I told myself it was probably just somebody working in a storeroom, but, in the subdued lighting of the souk, I could feel my pulse quickening as reason struggled to stay its ground. When, a short while later, I once again emerged on to Straight Street, away from the mass of people and the thick, scented air of the spice market, it seemed as if I had been granted a reprieve from the darker recesses of my own imagination.

'Hello! Hello!'

It was the young man from the nut and dried fruit shop, enthusiastically beckoning me across. I felt a strange sense of relief to see a familiar face. After a moment's hesitation, I walked over to where he was standing, his slim form squeezed into a pink T-shirt and a pair of the tight, faux-designer jeans that seemed so popular here.

'Try these, my friend,' he said, pushing a few pistachios into the palm of my hand. 'They are from Iran. The best!'

I cracked open the shells and began tasting the little green nuts.

'Yes? You like them?' he gave an appealing smile. 'Where are you from?'

'I'm British,' I replied, after a brief pause, wondering how he would react.

'Manchester United!' he grinned. 'You like Manchester United?' I was not sure if his enthusiasm was real or merely sales banter, but he seemed to take it in his stride when I said football was not quite my thing.

I bought half a kilo of pistachios and now had two bags to carry: the dried roses and the nuts. Dipping occasionally into the latter, and, somewhat irrationally, feeling reassured after the brief conversation, I continued my stroll and contemplated the long history of the narrow street with its modest architecture. Perhaps Saint Paul had also once stopped to buy pistachios from a street vendor all those centuries ago, I mused. Once again, here in Damascus I felt the sensation of continuity derived from the banal: everyday actions we repeat, as did countless generations before us, which link us to our past in a way that mere masonry and stonework cannot. As I walked along lost in my thoughts, an art shop suddenly caught my eye. Pausing to look in the large window, I wondered how I could have missed it earlier. Two paintings, one of what looked like a Damascene street scene, the other a still life with fruit, were propped on easels surrounded by an assortment of *objets d'art*. Yet it was not the paintings that caught my eye, but a marble bust on the floor between them. A strange mixture of the modern and the traditional, it was evidently new, though at once evocative of ancient Assyrian art, famous for its stone reliefs of human-headed winged lions and bulls. I looked at the long, angular face of the bust, the beard carved with deep-cut swirls; the thin, unseeing eyes little more than two lines, a stark contrast to the generous, almost pouting, lips. My eyes drifted to the sharp patterns of the carved headdress, deliberately broken off on one side at an angle. I was intrigued, I was tempted, and I knew exactly where in my house I could put it. For a while, I just stood gazing at the bust. The more I looked at it, the more I liked it and felt drawn to it. Suddenly, reflected in the shop window, I saw a dark figure, hands in pockets, leaning against a wall on the other side of the street behind me. A wave of nervousness slid over my body, cold even in the warmth of the Syrian afternoon: I was sure it was the same man I had seen before. Paranoia now gained the upper hand, choking off any rational thoughts. I decided to seek refuge in the shop.

Closing the door behind me I felt, illogically, as if I had reached sanctuary amidst the art. I looked around at the hotchpotch of paintings, some hanging in frames, others stretched over canvases and stacked against the rough stone walls. Smudged women reclined in the cooler corners of the shop, a strange contrast to alpine landscapes in thick oils and abstract compositions of lines and circles. There appeared to be no theme to the gallery, but all the works seemed recent and, in some, one could see the hand of the same artist.

'*Bonjour!*' said the gallery owner, rising from a wooden chair next to a desk covered with stacks of papers. Brushing crumbs from his shirt, he began to make his way carefully past the obstacle course of canvases that were leaning against various tables.

'*Bonjour!*' I replied, somewhat surprised. Although Syria had been part of the French Mandate between the wars, the thin-haired man now approaching was the first person here to address me in the language of Molière; in neighbouring Lebanon, half the country seemed to speak French. He adjusted the gold-rimmed glasses that sat on the bridge of his broad nose before looking me up and down. I imagined the man outside observing me just as closely.

'*Vous êtes français, monsieur?*'

'*Non, je suis anglais mais j'habite en Belgique,*' I replied.

'Ah! English!' His eyes flared a little and his eyebrows, two unkempt lines of fur, arched momentarily. 'Welcome to my gallery. You are interested in Syrian art? As you can see, I have a lot of fine things here. Come, let me show you something: I have a beautiful painting by a local artist that I think you will like. Syrian art is becoming very popular, you know.'

'Actually, I wanted to ask the price of the bust,' I said, turning to point a hand towards the statue, just visible from where we were standing. Now facing the window, I discreetly looked towards the street. The man with his hands in his pockets was still there, but, looking at him directly rather than merely seeing his reflection, I could see more clearly. He was wearing a black shirt, not a navy polo top. I felt my shoulders relax as I realised I had never seen him before: dazzling sunlight, strange shadows and preconceived ideas were potent fuel for the imagination in the ancient streets of Damascus.

'Ah, that! It's lovely, isn't it?' said the gallery owner, wiggling his fingers in mid-air as if about to help himself to a display of cakes. 'It's also by a local artist. Would you like to look at it?' He lifted to one side a portrait of a woman sketched in a style that had echoes of Picasso and moved a table with a collection of reclining grey figurines. Walking over to the bust, which was almost a metre high, he bent down, and, with a bit of a struggle, managed to lift it and carry it over to where I was standing. Setting it down carefully in front of me, he dusted off his hands with a cloth that was lying on a table and then wiped his brow. I crouched down and ran my fingers gently over the cool marble, in parts smooth like the floor of the Great Mosque, elsewhere rough as the day it was hewn. The motionless head was impervious to my caresses. Its exaggerated length and stylised features embodied it with a strange elegance. Here, before me, was something even more ancient than this city: the stone was literally as old as the hills. But I was curious as to something much more recent: the thoughts of the sculptor. What, I wondered, had inspired him to take a chunk of our planet and fashion from it this piece of art to create an intriguing take on antiquity?

'Perhaps you would like some tea?'

I looked up to see the rather portly gallery owner peering down at me through his spectacles and holding a round tray with two little glasses on it.

'Thank you,' I said, rising to my feet. The tulip-shaped glass was hot to the touch, steam rising from the copper-coloured brew. I took a sip; it was strong and very sweet.

'You like it here in Syria?'

'Yes,' I nodded. 'The people are very friendly.'

'Then I am sure you would like to take something back to your country with you,' he smiled.

'It's interesting,' I said, pondering the statue, 'but I couldn't possibly carry it on the plane back to Belgium.'

'But, *monsieur*, it is not a problem: we can ship it for you!'

When Mr al-Abboud said he would 'ship' the statue, I took his word literally and envisaged it on board a boat sailing across the Mediterranean and through the Straits of Gibraltar before picturesquely ploughing its way up the Spanish and French coasts until it reached Antwerp. Not for a moment did I imagine he would post a 45-kilo stone bust by airmail.

I look at the statue staring blindly up at me with the two slit eyes, sightless lines carved into mottled cream marble. I feel a wave of excitement that this most unusual of holiday mementos has arrived after its long journey. Pulling back more of the straw, I inspect it to make sure that it is not damaged. Everything is fine. Anton and I lift the bust out of its crate and carefully carry it up the main staircase where an empty niche is waiting for the new arrival. The statue is a perfect fit and silently takes up its place. The angular features and the long beard are unmistakably modern, yet allude to a Syria of many, many centuries ago. The country from which I have just returned is very different from how I imagined. I have no illusions about the regime, but the people themselves showed me nothing but friendliness. The impression so often conveyed of widespread hostility to the West was not borne out by my experience and I returned from Syria with a changed view of the country. In a way, I have had my own little Damascene conversion. I look at the bust and know that every time I go up and down stairs and see it I will think of that trip, of the city where history and belief are inextricably intertwined, of the welcoming people of Damascus. I decide to call the bust Saul.

What Lies Beneath

The letter Q must always be followed by a U. At least that is what I had always thought. Qatar was the first exception to the rule that I encountered as a young child. As in the case of another country on the Arabian Peninsula, I first became aware of the tiny state through my stamp collection. Qatar's philatelic output made a particularly colourful contribution to my favourites with its depictions of exotic beasts such as oryxes and camels. The inexplicable spelling of the country's name prompted me to demand an explanation from my parents. I do not recall any coming, but I remember I remained fascinated with the strange land whose postal authorities seemed to stand in defiance of everything teacher had told me. The sense of mystery was heightened by it being the only country in the whole wide world whose name began with the seventeenth letter of the alphabet, one so rarely used that, like Z, there was but a single tile in my favourite game, Scrabble, where managing to use it merited ten points. The seed of interest was sown. For a long time, I pronounced the state's name with the emphasis on the second syllable, making it sound like an unpleasant flu symptom and only years later, when the diminutive but activist state began to make television news headlines, did I discover that political correctness and squeamishness seemed to have rebranded the country to sound inoffensively like someone employed to catch domestic felines.

I first visited Qatar, on some counts the country with the highest per capita income in the world, many years later on the way to Yemen, a state languishing at the other end of the development scale. Even as I was busy building up my boyhood collection of worthless stamps, these two countries were already going along very different economic paths. In 1940, prospectors had struck oil in what was then the tiny British Protectorate of Qatar and black gold was rapidly transforming the former pearl fishing peninsula. The discovery of vast gas reserves three decades later provided another boost until, today, the barren sands of what passes there for countryside stand in abject contrast to the opulent glass and steel towers along the crescent-shaped waterfront of Doha, the Qatari capital. The flowing oil means the government has money to lavish on its quarter of a million citizens, providing them with free health care and education in a fiscal paradise devoid of income tax and VAT. But it also has endless cash reserves to pay for energy-intensive desalination plants that make seawater drinkable. In this arid emirate, water, perhaps the region's most precious resource, is free for all.

Yemen, meanwhile, is still the poor cousin for whom the outlook remains bleak: in the Land of the Queen of Sheba, the aquifers are sinking as quickly as water disappears into sand and there is no money to pay for hi-tech alternatives. And, while Qatar is busy using its wealth to punch above its weight on the world scene by doing everything from supporting Libyan rebels to hosting the Al Jazeerah TV network, on the other side of the Arabian Peninsula, Yemen's slide into ever deeper poverty has been accompanied by the struggle to fend off Al Qaeda.

As my plane prepared to land in Doha, the economic cleavage between the two countries was not, however, at the forefront of my mind. My attention was focused on the uninspiring view from the aircraft window: a flat sandy realm over which ran a vague network of roads and tracks, some little more than sketched outlines, work in progress like Qatar itself. Low buildings, many the colour of the ground as though camouflaged, dotted the bleak and barren landscape. As a child, I had never imagined I would one day set foot in this far-off country and now, despite the unappealing scene through the porthole, as the airplane's shadow grew larger, I began to feel a warm glow of excitement at finally fulfilling a dream.

The airport was being rebuilt at great expense and so, amidst a mixture of apologies for the current inconvenience and fanfares about the glory to come, the well-drilled crew dealt us coloured cards depending on whether we were in transit, merely using Qatar Airways' home base as a hub, or actually intending to enter the country. The lucky few who had opted for the limousine service were deplaned like royalty, while the rest of us were ferried to the distant airport buildings in long buses. At the transit terminal, everyone except myself and a ruddy-faced man in his fifties poured off, pushing their way through the glass doors of the building like sales-shoppers desperate to be first to snatch the best bargains. A few minutes later we reached the arrivals hall, vast and almost empty, with rows of immigration officials wrapped in perfectly ironed Arab robes, the men in long white *dishdashas*, the women in flowing black *abayas*, patiently waiting at their booths for a passenger to turn up. A short while later, with a new stamp and visa in my passport and baggage collected, I was in a taxi heading towards my hotel, passing cranes, reinforced concrete skeletons and glittering realisations of architects' dreams. Things were looking up.

Apart from the country itself, my main point of interest in Qatar was Doha's recently opened Museum of Islamic Art. I cannot pretend to be a specialist in the sphere, but the museum's collection was already the subject of international acclaim and a 'must see' on any visit to the country. It was only a short walk from my hotel, but striding over high kerbs and negotiating my way across unfinished pavements was not what I had expected. I picked my way towards the sea front, doing my best to stay in whatever shade there was to avoid the glare of the Arabian sun. As I rounded a corner, the museum came into sight, a stack of cream-coloured boxes rising out of the waters of Doha Port. I.M. Pei, the Chinese-American architect of Louvre pyramid fame who designed the place, wisely insisted that his creation stand on its own island to set it apart from other buildings. Walking slowly up the causeway to what appeared to be a virtually windowless structure, a double row of well-tended palm trees standing on either side, it was easy to imagine one had been transported back in time to some ancient civilisation with the path leading to the palace of its munificent leader. As I got nearer, lines of round Islamic arches came into view, softening the building's cubist style and hinting at the nature of the treasures within.

Inside, in darkened rooms, behind glass, glistened wonders of gold; wonders of gold among swirls of calligraphy, folds of silk, carvings of ivory and sets of ceramics. Here were the finest examples of centuries of Islamic art from lands as diverse as Spain and Turkey, China and Iran, countries in many ways different, yet bound together by the common thread passing through Mecca. It would have been easy to create a collection so vast as to overwhelm the visitor by its sheer size, to produce a sensation of smallness when confronted with such wonders, to mirror the very meaning of the name of the revered religion itself: submission. Yet the museum in Doha has taken a different approach, choosing instead to display a modest amount of exhibits of exceptional quality. I meandered from room to room, listening to the audio guide, transported to other worlds by the chocolate voice and the riches around me. Together with the black walls of the galleries, the clean lines and understated decor of the building – a rare feature in this part of the world –

discreetly accentuated the intricacy and detail of the objects on display. Stopping to marvel at a jewel-encrusted falcon, countless precious stones set into its golden form, I imagined it could have been lifted straight from a fairy tale about a powerful caliph offering the hand of his daughter in marriage to anyone who could make a fantastic creature of this kind. As a child, I used to devour such stories, running headlong into the colourful worlds of heroes and adventure they described. That the seventeenth-century artefact was actually from India only added to the exoticism, rulers in these legends often filling their palaces with fabulous treasures from far and wide. Like latter-day characters from one of Scheherazade's tales, the country's ruling Al-Thani family have spent fortunes on amassing the museum's collection, as if magically transforming the thick black liquid and invisible gas brought forth from beneath the Qatari earth into an Aladdin's cave of magnificent art.

As I was admiring the glistening raptor, I became aware that a man standing at my side was looking at me and saying something.

'I'm sorry?' I said, pulling the headphones of the audio guide away from my ears.

'It's fabulous, isn't it?' he smiled. 'The craftsmanship: it's exquisite.'

With his short dark hair and swarthy features he looked Middle Eastern, but there was something about him that made me think he was not an Arab: perhaps it was the bulbous nose or the small chin. I reckoned he was in his late thirties, but with the subdued lighting it was hard to be certain.

'Yes, I was just admiring it,' I agreed. 'In fact, the whole place is pretty spectacular.'

'You like Islamic art?

'I don't have a special interest in it, if that is what you mean,' I shrugged, 'but it would be difficult not to be impressed by the things in here.'

'Is this your first visit?' He cocked his head slightly to one side, the light from the display case showing up his heavy stubble.

'Yes,' I nodded, 'first time in the museum, and in the country. What about you? Are you from here?'

'No,' he laughed quietly. 'I'm not. Can't you tell? You wouldn't find a Qatari walking around Doha dressed like this! I'm Lebanese.'

Indeed, his striped shirt and sandy-coloured chinos were not typical Arab attire. We moved away from the glass case with the falcon so a young Arab couple could get a better view.

'You are on holiday here?'

'Sort of: more passing through. I've always wondered what Qatar was like and thought I would stop off to see. And you?'

'I work here. Not all the time, but I come quite often.'

'I see,' I said, wandering over to a display case where a collection of ornate rings was laid out, each one a tiny work of art. The man drifted after me and then stood by my side looking at the jewellery.

'They are so beautiful.'

He ran his fingers over the glass, as if trying to make some form of spiritual contact with the centuries-old jewels on the other side. The simple band of gold round his wedding finger came a poor second to the filigree and craftsmanship that lay just beyond reach. He seemed to become lost in his thoughts as he stared at the masterpieces glowing gently under the perfectly positioned spotlights.

I slipped away into the shadows and onwards to the next room where I stopped to study a pair of blue and white *Albarelli* – porcelain jars for storing medicines. In warm tones, the voice on my audio guide recounted how cylindrical pots like these from Damascus were in use in the Levant long before they were adopted in Europe and given an Italian name. As I turned away, an elderly tourist with a dowager's stoop gave a brief smile as she shuffled by, milky eyes making her look like a figure from a past era revisiting the present.

Knobbly fingers clutched a guidebook and what looked like a pile of scrawled notes that had been dropped and hastily gathered back together. Only her casual clothes and Birkenstock-style sandals gave any indication that she belonged to the here and now.

I moved on, exploring one angular chamber after the other, walking over geometric shapes cast on the floor by the miniature spotlights that shone through the glass cabinets. I stopped in front of a show case to admire a bluish-green glass bowl, traces of gold round its rim. After surviving many turbulent centuries, the fragile dish from Egypt had finally found refuge, a place to rest and bask in the adoration of its beauty. Surrounded by the dark walls of the exhibition rooms, the artefacts on display lay like pieces of hidden treasure, waiting, as if by some strange sorcery, to convince each set of eyes that fell upon them that they were the first to do so. A deep-blue page from a Koran seemed to positively glow, the intensity of its colour drawing me over as soon as I entered the room. Across its width were shining golden letters, stylised Arabic calligraphy that could have been an art deco interpretation of the normally florid swirls were it not for the fact that the page was over a thousand years old. In one room, portraits of nineteenth-century sheikhs locked in rigid poses, elegant beards stretching to their waists, watched me with cold, black eyes as I crept past, an infidel violating their jealously guarded hoard. In another, silk carpets flattened against the walls looked as if they might spring to life at any moment and begin flapping against the glass that protected them, as if desperate to escape, to fly away. The exhibits were truly fantastic, but, by the time I finished the tour, even in the coolness of the museum, my thoughts were becoming feverish.

I left the shadowy chambers and made my way down one of the twin staircases that curved their way into the atrium. It was on a very different scale to the exhibition rooms and flooded with daylight by floor-to-ceiling windows. At the bottom, I looked up to admire the cavernous space around me, letting my eyes follow the lines of sand-coloured walls that gradually became ceiling, seamlessly merging modern geometric design with traditional Islamic patterns, continuing ever higher until finally forming an octagonal dome. I craned my neck to look at the layers of triangles that repeated until the almost circular opening at the top through which sunlight fell. It was as if the entire cupola were a cut diamond of immense proportions: Pei had managed perfectly to evoke the fantastical world of the Arabian Nights through the medium of the most contemporary architecture.

'It's very well done, isn't it?' came a voice.

I turned to see the Lebanese man from earlier on. I could hardly disagree.

It was only as we walked over to the cafeteria that I noticed he had a slight limp, a poignant reminder, I felt sure, of his country's civil war. We each bought a coffee and a small bottle of water before sitting down at one of the little round tables. As the familiar aroma drifted up from our cups, the man introduced himself as Michel.

'So, did you like the museum, then?' I asked, taking a sip of my coffee. It was astonishingly good, rich like liquid velvet; I savoured the intense, nutty flavour as it seeped over my tongue.

'Yes,' he nodded, a touch of foamed milk on his lips. 'A wonderful collection. I've never had the chance to come before: I've always been too busy.' His dense eyebrows dipped a little while his eyes, two black marbles, remained fixed on mine.

Michel told me he worked for a hotel chain. He was based in Beirut, but spent most of his time travelling in the region. He was 32, married and had two children, a boy and a girl. He had been brought up a Christian, but had stopped believing in God ever since his motorcycle accident in Sidon in the south of the country. He had a brother in Toronto, another in New York and was allergic to tomatoes.

In the time it took to finish my coffee, I felt I had heard his entire life story: a little conveyer belt of factoids pouring out in some meaningless flow. I could not think of anything to say and there was nothing left to ask.

'How long are you in town for?' With his tanned fingers he gently pushed his coffee cup away.

'Just a couple of days,' I replied.

'I go back tomorrow,' he said, sitting back in his chair and placing his hands on a paunch I had not noticed before.

I glanced around the atrium; it was busier than I had realised. Tourists stared out of the windows while Arabs in flowing robes played with their mobile phones or tried to keep children under control. I took a swig of water to rinse the taste of coffee from my mouth.

'Do you enjoy working here?' I asked, suddenly thinking of a question.

'It's OK,' Michel shrugged, 'but it becomes boring after a while. It's quite claustrophobic. The expat society here exists behind a veil of civility, but if you scrape below the surface a bit you find that beneath the smiling façade they are all… well, bitchy.'

For a second, I was surprised he was so direct, but, given he had provided such a detailed exposé of his own life just moments before, I realised it was to be expected.

'I think it's because they all live on top of each other,' he said, twirling his coffee spoon between his fingers. 'In a manner of speaking…' he smiled, looking straight at me. 'They are like slaves.' He drew the last word out as if stretching a tired muscle.

'What do you mean?'

'Expats working here have to give up their passports to their employer. Of course, the government passed a law a while back making it illegal, but it still happens. So once you are here, you are stuck. Nearly everyone has to do it. You even have to apply in writing to get permission to leave. Your *kafeel* is responsible for you, but they also control you.'

'*Kafeel*?'

'Your sponsor – the person who employs you, organises a work visa, gives you somewhere to live. But you can't leave or change job without their permission.' He raised his eyebrows. 'You look surprised.'

'Are you just talking about domestic staff or…'

'No, I'm talking about everyone,' Michel interrupted. 'Not just Philippina maids or people working in restaurants: people in nice offices with expensive cars – it's the same for them. Sure, they earn a nice tax-free salary here, but everything in life has its price.' He looked at me probingly. 'Doesn't it?'

Clearing my throat, I gave a small shrug of the shoulders.

'Do you know a lot of people here?'

'Some – enough.'

For a moment, neither of us said anything.

'Well, it was nice to meet you,' I smiled.

'Likewise,' he nodded, pressing his lips together.

We stood up and said our goodbyes, casual, but slightly awkward. I watched as he turned and walked towards the gift shop.

I decided to take a look at the museum's courtyard just beyond the atrium. Shallow pools were the only decoration and, as I stepped outside, I was greeted by air that was as warm as that of the interior was cool. I stopped to contemplate the series of arches that ran the length of one side, slate-grey *voussoirs* and piers around their frames contrasting with the sandy stone of the wall above. The simplicity of style made a perfect frame through which to view the skyscrapers rising out of the haze on the other side of the man-made bay. Yet, despite imaginative designs and expensive materials, neither glass nor steel sparkled through the opaque voile that hung above the waters separating us. A handful of *dhows*, their romantic allure diminished by the faint hum of modern engines, made their way slowly between the shores. I centred one of the arches in the viewfinder of my camera, hoping to capture the contrast between its minimalist lines and the *arriviste* forest of architectural ostentation beyond. Of a contrast between old and new, there was no question: in Doha there is no old and the new grows almost as fast as plants in a speeded-up nature documentary. I snapped a few shots before pausing to contemplate the Manhattan-like cityscape across the bay, wondering how the scene might have been all those years ago when I first became aware of the country with the rebellious spelling. Perhaps in those days the wild beasts featured on my stamps really did wander the land.

A while later, I was standing on the nearby Corniche Promenade that ran along the waterfront watching a bright-red powerboat in the middle of the bay roar past at great speed, 'F1' emblazoned on its side. A spray of water flew behind it as it marked a broad curve and then raced back to where a group of men was gathered at the water's edge. The noise was incredible, the purpose dubious. The Qataris had come a long way since their life as desert nomads, I thought as the boat set off again, its motor blasting out like a heavy rock band that only plays one note. After watching for some time, I turned and headed back along the esplanade, my clothes sticking to me in the late afternoon heat. Lush lawns separated the broad pathway from the Corniche Road, a vivid band of soft green between hard beige paving and sticky black tarmac. Elsewhere, something as simple as grass would be so commonplace as to be virtually invisible; here, it was an artificial construct requiring constant life support. The emerald football pitches needed for the 2022 World Cup would, I thought, no doubt soak up enough water to supply a small town.

Ahead, a family of four from the subcontinent was marvelling at a model of a giant oyster in the centre of a round, rock-filled pond, their uniformly white sneakers bright in the sun. Water cascaded from the open shell that cradled an imitation pearl the size of a large beach ball, a reminder of the country's previous incarnation centred on its rich oyster beds. The parents were taking it in turns to photograph each other with the young son and daughter, who grinned broadly each time they were carefully positioned in front of the oversized mollusc. I asked if they would like me to take a picture of them all together and, a moment later, the family was lined up, a beaming example of India's burgeoning middle class. The slim, smartly dressed quartet stared unflinchingly while I clicked away. As I handed the camera back to the father, they quickly gathered round to check my efforts on the monitor.

'Ooh, that is very nice. Thank you!' smiled the woman, as the son and daughter strained to see the images.

'Can I take one of you with the children?' asked her husband. His thin moustache and shiny, carefully combed hair gave him an earnest look. I imagined him being an IT manager in Bengaluru.

I positioned myself between the boy and the girl with the bay as the backdrop and smiled while their father took a picture. He showed me the result, shading the camera's screen from the sun with his hand. I was surprised to see how small we were – barely half the height of the photograph – but nodded approvingly before saying goodbye and wishing them a nice holiday.

Continuing slowly on my way, I crossed over the busy Corniche Road and walked towards the Souk Waqif where rows of silver and white Land Cruisers and other huge 4x4s were parked in front of a series of low, unattractive buildings. I found myself a few paces behind a group of women heading in the same direction, their fluttering black *abayas* trailing on the dusty ground. Women are not exactly a rare sight here, but the multitude of mostly male expat workers, both blue- and white-collar, means women make up little more than a quarter of the population. The Qataris themselves are in the minority, foreigners outnumbering them nearly six to one.

As I approached the souk I was unsure what to expect, but any notions I may have had of still finding anything like an authentic bazaar were quickly laid to rest. Once the place where Bedouin tribesmen came to sell their goats, sheep and wool, I discovered the sometime traditional market had been given a makeover worthy of a TV home renovation show and more resembled a theme park reproduction than the genuine article. Wooden beams protruded from rendered walls, the original construction now concealed beneath a pseudo-rustic veneer of dried mud. Coffee shops with smart canvas sunshades and eateries offering chicken wings, hummus and pizza stood alongside antique shops and purveyors of fine souvenirs. Brass lamps of the sort a genie might one day pop out of dangled above rows of decorative plates and strings of colourful beads hung next to stacks of folded T-shirts. Yes, there were spices and the occasional *shisha* as well to add a sprinkling of authentic flavours and a waft of oriental aromas, but the environment was devoid of the character – and the characters – that make many of the souks of the Middle East so fascinating. It was not surprising given that, historically, Doha was never a great trading centre like Damascus or Baghdad. Founded only in the early part of the nineteenth century, for a long time it remained a fishing village and a base for pearling boats. For centuries, the small peninsula that is Qatar was a dusty open space, the oyster beds below the surface of the jade waters of the Gulf its only apparent source of wealth. Since time immemorial desert tribes herded their livestock across the bare landscape and sailors navigated boats over the sea in blissful ignorance of what lay beneath.

Today, the country is unimaginably rich and yet the value of Qatar's oil and gas resources is only as great as the technical and economic need for them: had they been discovered four hundred years ago, the lack of technology to extract them and put them to good use would have rendered them of little value. Ancient Mesopotamia, in contrast, prospered because its soils were fabulously fertile. Even with their basic tools and methods, the Bronze-Age farmers in the lands between the Euphrates and Tigris reaped upwards of thirty seeds for every one they sowed: their counterparts in Ancient Greece could only count on seven, those in Rome but four. Sandy Qatar is not intrinsically wealthy, I realised: it is functionally wealthy.

I stopped to look at some kilims and saddle packs set out on the ground, briefly enjoying the current of air flowing from the wall-mounted fans above before moving on at the sight of the shop owner scuttling towards me. I passed tables outside empty restaurants and terraces of cafés where a few Westerners, expats and tourists, some tanned, some red, sat drinking mint tea and soft drinks. Four young men in dazzlingly white *dishdashas* strolled towards me, laughing and chatting, a walking advert for washing powder or perhaps just extras volunteering to add a touch of authenticity. Their perfectly trimmed beards, black designer sandals with gold motifs and wedge-heels, and expensive, chunky watches told of an easy life, their carefree manner of the confidence that comes with wealth. As they passed me, their eyes and thoughts concealed behind dark glasses, I pondered the ease with which their manicured hands held each other, expressions of male friendship that would make many straight men in the West shudder, such is their fear of same-sex contact. Perfume floated in the warm air, expensive, unknown notes taunting the most primal sense, and smiles as white as freshly laundered *keffiyehs*, the traditional headscarves, appeared between perfect lips.

I continued walking along the flawlessly paved street, past neon calligraphy and quaint shop signs in French. Uninspired by souvenirs, postcards and lines of maroon and white Qatari flags, I turned and ambled back the way I had come. A lively squawking and chirping coming from a side street caught my attention. I wandered into it to find blue and orange macaws chained to perches, intelligent eyes observing every move around them. Rows of captive song birds, finches and canaries fluttered behind bars, while masses of tiny chicks huddled in cages, their feathers sprayed all colours of the rainbow, a horror that also used to happen in southern Europe until shockingly recently. The poor hatchlings would be sold not as pets but as toys, their lives unpleasant and short, their deaths long and lingering. I quickly left the bird market and returned to the main drag. Perhaps in the cool of the evening the souk would be busier, but at the moment it seemed like a holiday resort out of season and out of place. Eventually, I found myself at the entrance to a passageway leading into a building with what appeared to be everyday shops selling the sort of products locals might buy, such as flour, tea and shiny kettles. Even here, though, there was a polished tidiness that left little room for the sort of atmosphere one finds in a traditional souk.

I contemplated the difference between the examples of high culture on display in the Museum of Islamic Art and the wares in the much-renovated market aimed at tourists and souvenir hunters. Such extremes can be found the world over, of course: the pinnacles of human artistic achievement on display in the Louvre or the British Museum cannot be compared to the everyday items for sale on the high streets of Paris or London. Here in Qatar, though, another contrast was at play. As I made my way out of the sterile souk, I reflected on how the fabulous wealth of this barren country enabled its rulers to play a role in regional politics and to provide its citizens with a standard of living far superior to that which many in the so-called developed world enjoy. But the money which flowed as freely as oil and was a lubricant to political stability did not make Qatar an exciting place. Despite the glitzy skyscrapers, flash cars and roaring speedboats, it was more Switzerland than

Saint Tropez. As a child, I mistook the strange spelling of the emirate's name as a sign of being rebellious, yet this country was anything but.

I found a low wall, mercifully in shade, and, sitting down, sought refuge from the heat and a respite for my feet, weary from traipsing round all day. After many years wondering what the country was like, my curiosity had finally been satisfied. I was glad to have been able to visit Qatar, whatever it was like. It was not the exotic land of my boyhood fantasies, but, since I first learnt of the place, both it and I had moved on, grown and developed. The path and the destination were not separate, I realised: they were two parts of the same adventure.

'You look tired,' said a voice.

I looked up. It was Michel.

A Dry Tide Coming

I was just seven years old when I first heard of Yemen and, like Qatar, it was a stamp that introduced me to the country. The name, together with a colourful picture of a hoopoe, was on an unfranked one I acquired for my collection. The strange, fan-like crown, fawn plumage and striped wings of the bird were as unfamiliar to a young boy in the drab North West of England as the name of the country. In the atlas I discovered it was next to Arabia. Arabia – the very word made the juvenile pulse race as it conjured up images of the exotic and the exciting, fuelled no doubt by the illustrations in a large book we had containing a selection of *Tales from the Thousand and One Nights,* specially adapted for children. Yemen must be a beautiful place to have such lovely stamps, I smiled, admiring my prize philatelic specimen held carefully between my small fingers. No, I was told, fancy stamps were just something poor countries sold to try to make money: it was probably horrible.

Despite the discouragement, I retained, somewhere at the back of my mind, a fascination with Yemen. Years later, when the opportunity to visit the country arose, I was again confronted with cold water being poured on my interest, this time by friends who, ensconced in their armchairs, hand-wringingly cautioned of the dangers that lurked there, of Al Qaeda and of the perils of kidnapping. Yet their well-meant warnings, informed by lurid newspaper articles, contrasted diametrically with the views of those people I knew who had actually visited the country: without exception, they thought it wonderful and acclaimed its people

among the friendliest they had ever met. I was determined to go.
Perhaps I would even see a hoopoe.

Now I am finally on a plane for Sana'a. It is March 2011; the Arab
spring that is blowing across Tunisia and Egypt like a *simoom* is
spreading to Libya and Yemen. Perhaps it is not the best time for
visiting the erstwhile Land of the Queen of Sheba, but in an area as
volatile as the Middle East, putting plans on hold until things calm
down is like waiting for Godot; besides, the way events are going, I
know this could be the last chance to visit the country for some
time. To be honest, despite all the praise from those familiar with
Yemen, against the background of growing civil unrest, it is not
without some trepidation that I find myself travelling to a country
renowned for tribal strife and widespread gun ownership where the
Kalashnikov is the weapon of choice.

During my plane's descent over the capital of Arabia Felix – or
'Happy Arabia', as the Romans and, later, geographers used to call
Yemen – I am struck by the size of the sprawling city. Extending far
beyond the ancient centre of Sana'a is a mass of ugly, modern
constructions. Low, sandy-coloured buildings stretch to the
mountains in one direction and as far as the eye can see in the other.
The monotony is broken only by the occasional tuft of dark green,
scrub-like vegetation. Not here the vivid emerald hues of those
cities where money is no object when it comes to making the desert
bloom: Sana'a's penury of water reflects Yemen's broader poverty
and its unenviable position as the Arab world's poorest country.

There is no motorway from the airport to the centre of this,
one of the planet's oldest continuously inhabited cities. Instead, my
taciturn driver, one hand on the wheel, the other holding his
cigarette just outside the open window, races and swerves along a

chaotic network of roads. At one point, we career off *piste* to bounce along undulating and potholed back streets. The way seems so unlikely to be the main route from the airport to the heart of the city that I wonder if I am already being kidnapped, destined to be delivered to my captors only minutes after arriving in the country. The tight feeling in my chest subsides, however, as, to my relief, we emerge from the desolate neighbourhood to rejoin a paved road. I cannot help thinking how much more difficult, not to say perilous, the circuitous route back to the airport would be if matters were to take a sudden turn for the worse. The hurried, haphazard nature of Sana'a's growth is evident everywhere: town planning is clearly a concept yet to arrive in Yemen. As I look at the dilapidated monochrome buildings, I reckon that if Eskimos have a hundred words for white, Yemenis must surely have at least as many for shades of beige. Dust is ubiquitous in this desiccated city, settling like some malevolent enchanted powder designed to keep the population under a spell of passivity. Yet, as we pass groups of soldiers and the occasional military vehicle, I wonder for how long the regime will be able to retain its grasp on power or whether the president's attempts to stand his ground will be about as effective as King Canute's commands to the sea.

After bumping and battling our way through the newer parts of Sana'a, we finally arrive at the historic centre. We approach it along As Sallah Street, a paved and walled *wadi*, or seasonal riverbed, that lies a few metres below the level of the surrounding land and that in the long dry period functions as a road. The taxi slows down and then turns on to a short but steep rise that leads back up to ground level and into the old town. The driver's cigarette has, I notice, disappeared somewhere along the way. The streets look too narrow to drive down, but somehow we squeeze through the rough-walled gullies without scraping the sides of the car. With resignation, the few pedestrians there are – sinewy, dusty figures –

step into doorways to avoid being crushed against the walls as we push our way past. We almost come to a halt while the driver negotiates his way over an angled row of collapsible metal teeth that stick up out of the road to prevent vehicles from driving the wrong way down the street, something the lawless Yemenis would surely otherwise do. Suddenly, the road opens out into a sort of misshapen plaza to the left of which stands my hotel. I peer out of the taxi window at the mud-brick building towering above me and try to count how many storeys it has.

A couple of hours later after a quick breakfast, I am out on the street, seeking refuge from the glare of the sun and staying, as much as possible, in the relative cool of the shadows that jut out from the high walls. In the modest square near the hotel, several vehicles, mostly light-coloured Toyotas and Suzukis, are parked with surprising orderliness. Plump women waddle slowly between the shops set in the base of the tower houses, so emblematic of Sana'a, later emerging from the shade of the tiny retail grottos with plastic bags bulging with vegetables and packets. Covered from head to foot in sombre black *sharshafs*, the typical outfits made up of cape, veil and pleated skirt, or occasionally draped in brightly patterned *sitaras*, the flowing robes unique to Sana'anis, they go about their business at a leisurely pace.

I set off to wander round the labyrinth of dusty streets to discover what is at 2,300 metres one of the world's highest capitals. Old Sana'a has the reputation of being a maze in which one can easily get lost. I am confident this will not happen to me, however: not only do I pride myself on my sense of direction, I am armed with two guidebook maps and a proposed walking tour in German that takes in the highlights of the old city. Yet cartographers, even German ones, are challenged by Sana'a with its irregular streets – one moment comprising broad paved areas, the next narrowing to become rough, sandy alleys – and its unevenly shaped buildings that defy anyone to describe them as city blocks. The more I look at them the more medieval and mystical the maps appear. In the absence of almost any street names the walking tour is based on footsteps: after 58 paces turn right, then 23 paces later go left, and so on, making my stroll round the city feel like a hunt for hidden treasure.

Before long, thirst catches up with me as the sun burns relentlessly in the clear sky. I spy a small shop selling a variety of groceries – cooking oil, bags of rice, and various other dry goods in sacks and packets. I head towards it to buy a bottle of water. On the wall next to the entrance a besuited President Saleh backed by a Yemeni flag stares out from a fresh poster. Inside, it takes a few moments for my eyes to adjust to the dark and for my nose to recognise the aromas of tea, coffee, turmeric and cloves. The middle-aged shopkeeper is chatting to a thin man seated on a wooden box, who is eating his way through a handful of pistachio nuts. I glance at their traditional Yemeni *ma'awazes*, a sort of striped sarong, and their grey, Western-style suit jackets that have seen better days. Their conversation comes to an abrupt halt as I enter and pick up a small bottle of water from a stack half a dozen bottles high. I turn to face the shopkeeper, of heavier build than his friend, and hold up my purchase.

'First time in Yemen?' he asks, as I hand over my *rials*. In the half-light he appears to be about my age, although in Yemen, as in many developing countries, looks can be deceptive: wrinkled, weather-beaten complexions tell of harsh living and life-long toil, a world removed from our own easy existences. As I often do, I find myself considering for a moment how his life will have differed from my own as, over the years, we have each walked this earth before finally coming together for this fleeting encounter. And I wonder what he was doing at the exact moment I first held that Yemeni stamp with its picture of the hoopoe and became aware of the existence of his country. Was he playing barefoot in the dry dirt? Or was he already working, perhaps labouring in a field under the hot Arabian sun, or peddling shoe laces on a crowded street in order to help the family budget? I would never know.

'Yes,' I nod, 'first time.'

'Welcome to Yemen!' he smiles, flashing a couple of gold teeth beneath his thick, slightly greying moustache. 'You like it here?'

His friend looks at me with an expression of mild curiosity on his chiselled face and cracks open a pistachio with a deftness that comes from years of practice. He has a lazy eye and I have the strange sensation that half his attention is focused on my ear. 'Yes, I do,' I say, deciding to keep my response simple.

'Yemen very safe!' declares the shopkeeper, as he hands me my change. 'But not many tourists now. Very bad!'

I do not know what to say: neither sympathy nor indifference seem appropriate.

'It's a pity,' I nod, after a slight pause, 'because Sana'a is very beautiful.'

'Ah, yes, it is a beautiful city,' he agrees, his eyebrows floating momentarily upwards.

A short silence follows, broken by the crack of another pistachio. I put my change away, thank him and then smile goodbye to the two men.

Back out on the street, I take a swig of my precious water, a rare commodity in this increasingly arid country. I know that Sana'a is drying out, and quickly. Its water table, once just fifty metres below ground, has now plummeted to a depth of over six hundred metres. And it is sinking by a further six to eight metres a year like water down a plug hole as the city's mushrooming population draws on it for its daily needs. I look at the plastic bottle in my hand: a quick-fix solution for drinking water, but what about supplying all the other needs such as water for washing? Experts forecast that by 2020 there will be no water left at all in Sana'a. The city, it is said, could be the first capital in the world to run dry, an ironic fate for a town reputedly founded by Noah's son Shem. Herein lies a challenge on such a scale that no street protest or change of government will be able to provide an easy remedy. Once again, it is like the sort of seemingly unsolvable problem that a sultan in one of the *Tales from the Thousand and One Nights* might have given to a suitor seeking his daughter's hand in marriage, but, whereas in such stories the hero is able to come up with a clever answer, the harsh reality facing Yemen is that a happy ending is unlikely. Here, it will take much more than a bejewelled bird to resolve the country's problems.

Wandering past stalls selling misshapen vegetables – carrots, potatoes, tomatoes – and limp herbs, their leaves withering in the sun, I look at the wizened men and hopeful boys sitting or standing patiently by their wares. I reflect on the paltry displays of goods, often not even enough to cover the wooden table or cloth on which they are set out, knowing that entire families will depend on their sale.

I continue to follow my maps and try to remember to count my paces, keeping an eye out for landmarks such as mosques and minarets that might help me find my way. Here and there, bougainvillea hangs over high walls, hinting at hidden or perhaps merely imagined gardens on the other side, while carved wooden doors tempt one to wonder what lies beyond.

Arriving at a small plaza, I pause to look at the tower houses. Leaning against each other at strange angles, it seems as if only mutual support is preventing them from collapsing and as though the slightest tremor would in an instant reduce their weary walls to dust and rubble. Up to eight or nine storeys high, they resemble ever smaller boxes stacked one on top of the other. The geometric patterns of whitewashed brickwork that transect the sandy-coloured buildings look like icing sugar decoration and the effect is such that, from a distance, one could be forgiven for thinking that the old city is made entirely of gingerbread. Rows of *qamariya*, the traditional windows with tiny, coloured glass panes squeezed between ornate patterned frames, also whitewashed with gypsum, look, from down at street level, like lacework. These, together with the elaborately crenellated walls around the flat roofs, serve to lighten the overall impression of this overtly vertical city. And between all these buildings hangs a cat's cradle of generations of power lines and wires. As a young boy living in a low-rise 1960s suburb under leaden skies, I could never have imagined such places, such buildings, existed, and that people actually lived in them. A beige bird flies in front of me and alights on the branch of a tree. For a moment, I think it is a hoopoe, but it is merely a dove. Its gentle cooing makes me realise I have no idea as to the song or call of the strange fowl on my childhood stamp.

As I continue exploring, every now and then I emerge from the warren of narrow alleys into one of the irregular open areas, which are like little oases of horizontality between all the high walls. Sometimes, when I walk into one of these, I feel as if I must be the first non-Yemeni to do so, such is the air of isolation and sense of discovery, even though I am in the middle of a densely populated metropolis. Small, barefoot children stop playing and stare, sometimes greeting me with a 'Hello! ' or *'Bonjour!'*. There are a lot of children in Sana'a: nearly half the country is under the age of fourteen. Over the past thirty years Yemen's population has increased tenfold: when I proudly stuck that stamp in my album, Sana'a was home to just 55,000 people; now nearly two and a quarter million Yemenis surround me as I wander the city's streets. The capital creaks under the strain of this staggering growth, brought about by migration from the countryside and the combination of improved medical care and the lack of sufficient cultural change needed to reduce family size. Today is International Women's Day, and a local

English language newspaper I perused over breakfast in the hotel ran an article on reproductive issues. Whereas parents used to have ten or twelve children and expected only two or three to survive, today Yemeni women bear on average 'only' seven; in Sana'a the number is nearer five, of whom most will make it to adulthood. Nevertheless, despite improvements in the country's healthcare, the starting point against which such progress is measured is very low and the situation remains dire. Statistically, the newspaper reported, one Yemeni woman in 39 will die in childbirth, one of the worst figures in the world. As I walk around the winding streets of this ancient city, I look at the children playing their simple games with balls and sticks and wonder what the future will hold for them both in the coming weeks and months, and in the years ahead.

After twice ending up in one particular 'square', I realise that the city has got the better of me after all, despite my careful step-counting. A group of small boys, slight in build and wearing grubby T-shirts and shiny football shorts, ask, in surprisingly good English, if I am lost. I do not want to admit it, partly through pride, and partly because I think they might lead me to some dead-end alley and then produce that most Yemeni of accessories, a *jambiya* or dagger, even at their tender age, although I reckon they are older than their small stature suggests.

'No,' I say. 'I am not lost, just looking for the Tawashi mosque.'

Without hesitation, a chorus of competing voices explains how to get there, but I am unconvinced by the direction in which they point me. I set off, pretending to believe them, cheerfully waving goodbye, but take a different path as soon as I am out of sight. A couple of minutes later, to my embarrassment, I find myself back where I started and staring at the same group of boys who now look at me as if I am a few camels short of a caravan for not having been capable of following their simple directions. This time, wondering if I am not taking my life in my hands, I agree to let them show me the way, which they do with an air of excitement and satisfied authority. A taller boy in the group takes hold of my forearm with his slender hand and begins to lead me along the dusty street, clearly eager to impress. His friends follow enthusiastically, watching my every move. In just a few years, I reflect, his willowy child's fingers will probably be used to holding a gun, innocence lost forever as they curl around the trigger.

'First time in Yemen?' he asks, his brown eyes glinting with enthusiasm. Clearly, this seems to be a standard question to put to foreigners.

'Yes,' I smile.

'You like Yemen?'

'Yes, it's very nice,' I nod, realising that my concerns for my personal safety are little short of delusional.

He grins at the answer. Some of the other boys whisper to each other and giggle. After a few turns down narrow streets and deep alleys, we are suddenly in front of the mosque. I thank my young guides, wondering whether to give a few *rials'* reward or whether to do so would simply encourage a begging mentality. They seem not to expect anything, however, and, without lingering, cheerfully scamper off in the direction from where we came, laughing and shouting to each other as they go.

From the mosque, it is just a few minutes' walk to the souk with its eclectic mix of dried fruit, shining brassware, spices, plastic household items, clothing, and, rather bizarrely, Tate & Lyle Golden Syrup, a clear favourite in Yemen; tins of a size one normally associates with emulsion paint are stacked pyramid-style at one stall after the other. A left-over from colonial times under the British, I wonder? Goods are piled high, but there are few shoppers. Here, life seems to be at a slower, almost meditative, pace. The men running the stores look at me with curiosity, their dark eyes shining. Occasionally, a flash of bright blue or green sparkles incongruously from one of the many tanned faces, a reminder of the importance of trade in Yemen's long history as part of the spice and incense routes. Every now and then, strange but friendly words float through the aromatic air, inviting me to taste a date or slice of fruit proffered between bony, chestnut-coloured fingers. In the afternoon heat, they flick their wares clean with grey feather dusters, chat with each other, or sit and chew *qat*.

I had read about *qat* before arriving, but the first time I see a man walk past me with a mouthful of it I assume he has some dreadful tumour, such is the bulge in the side of his cheek. Only when I see several more men with the same feature do I realise that the lump is not some widespread carcinoma, but the usual way to take the drug. Yet, if it is not a physical affliction, it is certainly a socio-economic one. Banned in neighbouring Saudi Arabia, *qat* is the drug of choice in Yemen. Its use is both traditional and extensive, although more men than women chew it. Looking somewhat like privet, the leaves produce a stimulant when chewed. The *qat* 'industry' employs four million Yemenis and turns the afternoons of millions more, including the police, into a mild, drug-induced state of euphoria as they chew the leaves for hours on end before spitting out the dark green pulp where it lies drying on the street, looking like boiled spinach. Vast areas of precious agricultural land and huge amounts of scarce water are dedicated to the production of this drug in a country that has to import most of its food. While it is a useful cash crop for farmers, *qat* represents a serious drain on the country's resources with many Yemenis spending between a quarter and a third of their income on it.

I take another swig from my bottle of water and continue my walk through the fortified city. The street begins sloping downhill slightly and I suddenly find myself overlooking a walled patch of vibrant green, one of the communal vegetable gardens that still remain in the densely built old town. It is easy to see why, in the parched lands of the Middle East, green should be the holy colour of Islam, symbolising as it does the triumph of life in what is often an inhospitable environment. A couple of palms and a few other trees stand guard over the carefully planted rows of what look like herbs and salad. Between them sway a few wild flowers as if put there by nature herself as a token gift to those who have so little.

I am one of those old-fashioned people who still send postcards when travelling and immediately bought a handful at the little shop in my hotel. Now, I need to buy stamps and so head to the main post office at Tahiya Square, the site of recent demonstrations. From the historic centre, it is a five-minute walk across a bridge spanning the moat-like As Sallah Street and along a couple of roads where, in comparison to the old city, the shops look modern with their displays of fake designer T-shirts, jeans and a lurid assortment of glittery tops and pullovers. Choking on exhaust fumes, I negotiate my way over a busy street, half of which is taken up by cars parked with an abandon that is in abject contrast to the neatness of those in the square next to my hotel. I make my way past the half-dozen or so policemen in blue uniforms, who are leaning nonchalantly against the metal barricades at the roadside watching the world go by. Eventually, I reach the post office with its distinctive bright yellow hoarding and walk in front of a tight row of men, young and old, sitting on the ground with their backs against the wall of the building. As if transported from the pictures in my guidebook, in their traditional long white *thobes* and with scarves tied round their heads, the men present a typical Yemeni image as they chew *qat* and casually chat to each other.

'Welcome to Yemen!' says one of the younger men, raising a hand as I walk past. He adjusts the red and white chequered scarf draped round his neck as if he is cold, a near impossibility given the temperature, and beams a smile that could get him a job advertising toothpaste.

'Thank you!' I nod, still a little surprised by the friendliness I encounter everywhere.

It is difficult to see much of Tahiya Square itself as demonstrators have set up a series of large tents from which loudspeakers blast out a mixture of music and political speeches. For now, the atmosphere is relaxed, almost festive, but I know that as and when things heat up this unremarkable square could end up being the crucible of a bloody revolution. Inside, the post office, its canary-yellow corporate colours now tempered with sombre grey, is surprisingly quiet. About half of the ten or so counters seem to be designated exclusively for pay-outs to the few men huddling round them or filling out forms; the rest are closed. Disorderly piles of papers lie on a couple of tables, other sheets and stubs, crumpled and discarded, litter the floor. I spot the stamp counter to my left; it is unmanned, but after a few moments a silver-haired official appears. His dark eyes look at me solemnly from behind his improbably large nose as he waits for me to say what I want. Not knowing how much English he speaks, I show him my six postcards and say 'Europe'. Outside, a voice bellows through the loudspeakers in declaratory but not aggressive style, the volume only partly muffled by the post office walls and windows. Whatever the orator is saying, the glum man in front of me pays no attention. Instead, opening a large bound book with the deference one might normally reserve for a medieval Koran, he carefully takes out a strip of stamps and with long fingers slips them under the security window that separates us. Bordered by a thick band of yellow, the stamps show a photographic view of old Sana'a; their modern and utilitarian appearance pales in contrast to the almost artistic beauty of my boyhood specimen. I pay my 600 *rials*; and as I stick the stamps on my postcards, I recall briefly the child I once was and sense a momentary flicker of satisfaction at having finally made this journey, even if the country's philatelic production is not what it used to be.

I hand the postcards to the official, who promptly throws them into a cardboard box on the floor before returning to the backroom area of the post office. I wonder whether my greetings will ever arrive at their destinations.

In the evening, back at the hotel, there is a wonderful view over the old town from the rooftop terrace. The 14,000 or so mud-brick buildings are packed so closely together that many of the city's narrow streets are in shadow for at least part of the day. I can see places that at street level are hidden from sight and surprisingly many patches of derelict land where children play and tired washing hangs out to dry. And, nestling on the rooftops, are dozens of satellite dishes through which is served a diet of images from the astonishingly different worlds of the Gulf states on the other side of the peninsula, and which act as a reminder that, beyond the city's ancient façades, the modern world is seeping into Sana'a.

As the Arabian sun sinks below the mountains that surround the city, darkness floats down on the parched jumble of buildings spread out before me and silhouettes of clouds begin slipping ominously across the dimming sky. Lights start to come on like fireflies and in the distance the recently completed Al-Saleh mosque, all $68 million worth of it, glows an unholy white under the glare of its illuminations, its six 100-metre-high minarets looking like the chimneys of some fantastic factory. All looks peaceful, yet I can still hear the declarations of the protestors just a few minutes' walk away in Tahiya Square, their words drifting through the warm evening air. The winds that are sweeping across the Arab world are coming to Yemen too: to the stout women I saw carrying their grocery bags, to the moustachioed shopkeeper who sold me my bottle of water, to the children who showed me the way, to the men sitting outside the post office. Presidential decrees will not hold back the current of change for much longer. The tide is coming in, but, in this country starved of water, it will be a dry one.

The stamp with the hoopoe is now but a memory, lost somewhere in the course of moves from one country to another. As for the bird itself, I never saw one during my visit to Yemen, but I did, after many years of waiting, experience the country. Yes, it is indeed poor, but it is also a beautiful place and its people disarmingly friendly. It is with pride that I can now add my voice to those who sing its praises. Sadly, though, Arabia Felix, I feel, is about to face unhappy times.

The Whore and the Potter

So, you want to know about Beirut? I shall tell you. And I shall tell you about Joseph.

Beirut is an assault on the senses: noisy, brash, chaotic, glossy, dusty, chic. You could fill a treasure chest with all the adjectives that apply to the Lebanese capital and still be left with your arms full: no description could ever really capture the nature or the spirit of this most vibrant of cities. It oozes sensuality, it tempts you with its materialism, it pulsates with oriental beats, and it makes you breathe a heady mix of perfume, sweat, *shisha* smoke and exhaust fumes, a concoction potent enough to cloud even the clearest of heads. I first visited Beirut a few years ago and was quickly swept up by its siren promises of all the desires and cravings we were always told to avoid.

It is easy to see why Beirut has been dubbed the 'whore of the East'. The city positively reeks of five of the seven deadly sins – lust, greed, pride, envy, and gluttony – with only wrath and sloth not immediately evident, the first simmering just below the thin veneer that has, so far, prevented a new outbreak of sectarian fighting and the latter reclining behind screens in luxurious apartments. Despite the profusion of religious buildings, there is scant evidence of Catholicism's seven virtues or Islam's even longer list of desirable qualities. Maybe, deep inside the cool shadows of the immaculate Maronite churches, one might find some traces of humility, but, outside their doors, fabulous jewellery and shiny black SUVs flash and glisten in the Mediterranean sunlight and the conversation is about money, not morals. Beirut is a whore and proud of it.

It is to this city that I now return for the second time. I find familiarity mutes the excitement I felt on previous visits: having already slept with the whore, I know what to expect and have developed immunity to her lures. Today, I am in search of art or, more precisely, the artist.

On my first visit to Beirut, I saw a large earthenware bowl decorated with fish displayed in the window of a disused shop. A small, hand-drawn map next to the dish indicated that the artist's workshop was just around the corner and I visited him to ask how much it was. The artist's name was Joseph.

I begin my walk to Joseph's atelier at Place Sassine, a small hilltop roundabout surrounded by global brand coffee houses and an eclectic mix of little local shops selling everything from cakes to watches. As at most important junctions in Beirut, tanned policemen in grey camouflage uniforms and mirror sunglasses hang around, semi-automatic weapons slung casually over their shoulders. You can almost see the testosterone rising from them like heat haze on a hot day.

I head downhill past the landmark ABC Mall, a beige concrete colossus that occupies an entire city block and acts as a social focal point for affluent Beirutis. Here, well-coiffed ladies of a certain age stroll accompanied, for no other reason than to display status, by submissive Philippina maids, while groups of elegant teenage girls with bandages across their noses glide around to show off their plastic surgery, a highly-prized graduation gift from doting parents. If vanity had a nationality, it would be Lebanese, and not without reason, for the Phoenicians are a beautiful people.

'Taxi?' calls one of the middle-aged drivers milling around outside the mall entrance. 'Taxi?'

Glancing across, I see his dark blue pullover stretched over a rotund gut and that, despite the sunshine, he is wearing a jacket that looks as tired as he does. Behind him, a beautiful woman with a diamond necklace looks down from a billboard above the words '*My jewel, My right*'.

I shake my head and the sales pitch stops. I carry on towards the narrow, shady streets of Achrafieh. Somewhere in this hillside warren is Joseph's atelier. It is a messy place, as befits an artist's studio.

I remember: he was standing shirtless at a washbasin shaving. I knocked on the glass door and he signalled for me to wait while he fetched the key. When I told him I was interested in the 'dish with the fish', his blue eyes lit up and he ushered me into the small work space, which was really a gutted empty shop with a mezzanine on top of which was a mattress where he slept. I recall that the place was overwhelmingly grey and that there were small stacks of plates and bowls, plus a few jugs, lying around. Their beauty was in their simplicity. I think the fish were blue; I remember they were $700.

Cars rush and roar their way past, their owners somehow managing to smoke, phone and drive all at the same time. Above the constant revving of engines and claxoning, though, are other, deeper noises: those of bulldozers, demolition balls, concrete mixers and cranes churning out a mechanical funeral dirge that comes at me from all directions. My heart sinks. Everywhere in Achrafieh, crumbling villas from the time of the French Mandate with magnificent mature trees in their gardens, rather like elderly aunts adorned with emeralds, are gradually being culled and replaced by brash, gleaming tower blocks, greenery trailing from their balconies and terraces like cheap costume jewellery.

Joseph was probably in his late thirties, but his skin bore the signs of an intensity of living that made him look at least a decade older. He was despondent about what was happening to his city. Speculators were destroying it, he sighed, running his rough potter's fingers through his hair. Soon there would be nothing left: no heritage, no culture; just glass, just shops. We talked more about the transformation of Achrafieh than about his art. The sparkle in his eyes when we talked about his work faded when we discussed what was happening to old Beirut.

'The politicians and the real estate developers all belong to the same families,' he shrugged, lighting a cigarette. 'Besides, what would you do if you had an old villa in need of expensive repairs, but you could sell it for $25 million to a developer?'

Deep down, I knew the answer.

'Beirut was once the 'Paris of the East',' he said, as if reading my thoughts.

I compared this to its other epithet and realised such contradictions lay at the heart of the city.

I stop to look at a concrete skeleton that looms over the honey-coloured façade of a three-storey house, the front and side walls now all that remain of a once elegant residence. A picture of the finished result – a luxurious skyscraper incorporating a small, yellow corner – is posted on hoarding in front of the building site alongside a text that enthuses about the harmonious marriage of the old and the new. I wonder what the workers who are involved in this wholesale destruction of the city think, but then I see a trio of lean and dusty men from the subcontinent filing out from the site. One by one, they each buy a loaf of unleavened bread from a gaunt man with a hand-pushed cart and then sit on the kerb to eat this, their lunch. I realise their priorities and their world are very different from yours or mine.

As we sipped mint tea in the coolness of the workshop, Joseph reflected on the irony that some of the city's most beautiful *quartiers* had been spared during conflict only to be destroyed in peacetime. And I recounted how, when I had told people I was going to Beirut, their reaction had been one of wide-eyed surprise, such was the power of the images of the Lebanese civil war even twenty years after it had ended.

Perhaps the images that stick in your mind are of burnt-out buildings and columns of smoke rising from rubble. True, there remain some scars of the war today: the iconic Holiday Inn still stands, an empty concrete shell pockmarked with bullet holes. Much of downtown Beirut has been rebuilt as a pastiche of former elegant shopping streets or as glistening towers reflecting the Mediterranean sun. The city's cosmopolitan Souk al-Tawileh, with its boutiques and perfumeries, and the Souk Ayass that sold clothes and textiles were both destroyed in the war, but have risen from the ashes in the form of the newly built Beirut Souks. The scent of flavoured lattes has replaced the smell of oriental spices, in-store piped music the tradesmen's cries. Yet, if you were to walk through the graceful arcades of this twenty-first-century reinterpretation of the old markets with its soft lighting and polished stone floors, smart boutiques and luxury brands, I am sure you, too, would get a sensation of the ephemeral – that it is but a matter of time before conflict breaks out again. Is this why Beirutis live for the moment, making money while they can? If you lived on a volcano, would not *carpe diem* be your motto?

I arrive at the window where I first saw Joseph's work displayed. There is no pottery, just funky lamps in orange and purple. With some trepidation, I continue to the workshop, but when I get there I find it is abandoned. I peer through the dirty window: there is nothing to suggest the place has ever been occupied and no sign to indicate that Joseph has moved on to bigger and better things. A shadow passes over me. I look up to see the arm of a crane swinging overhead with a load of prefabricated concrete blocks. I never bought anything from Joseph. I regret it.

You want me to tell you about Beirut? I cannot: I told you, there are no words to describe it. You must come and see for yourself, soon.

White on Blue

The reality suddenly hits me and I wonder if I have not embarked on true folly. I do a double-take as I look out of the aeroplane window and feel my stomach tighten. Between the rolling, khaki-coloured hills with patches of snow still dotting their tops and my Turkish Airlines Airbus flies a drone, its strange, grey form like some giant winged tadpole gliding malevolently above the barren countryside, waiting to strike. I keep my nose pressed to the porthole as we fly ever lower, the outskirts of the city finally coming into view: row upon row of shipping containers, army stores and prefabs are gradually replaced by a jumble of tiny, flat-roofed houses clinging to the hillsides and then stretching across the plain that lies surrounded by the mountains of the Hindu Kush. As we land, feelings of regret churn with a sensation of excitement as I see lines of military airplanes and helicopters. Eventually, a civil craft comes into view, but there is no doubt about it: Kabul Airport is unlike any other I have been to.

Everyone files out of the plane. I look around at the mostly male passengers and wonder what brings them here. I imagine the big, muscular guys with crew cuts are private security; the small, skinny ones employees of Western governments or the ubiquitous non-governmental organisations, the NGOs. Perhaps there is a journalist or two among them; I suspect I am the only tourist. The airport building is shabby and dusty, despite signs proclaiming its recent renovation. I wonder what state it was in before. I get the relevant stamps on the right bits of paper, wait nervously for my luggage, am surprised when it appears, and then queue to show my passport to indifferent officials. Everything goes surprisingly smoothly and sooner than expected I find myself outside, squinting in the cold March sunshine. A perfect blue sky, a crisp morning, a handful of birds flying an arc above: here was the innocence of nature against the backdrop of violence that has marred this city for years.

All I have to do now is follow the little map I was sent by e-mail and make my way to the perimeter fence where James is waiting to meet me. For security reasons, only passengers are allowed into the airport buildings: everyone else has to stay outside. All the people from my flight are trooping off in the same direction, so I simply follow them across empty car parks and through open gateways, wheeling my duffel bag behind me. At the final gate, there is a baffling sign saying '*Switch Your Jammer Off*'. A crowd of perhaps two dozen waits; among the tanned and wizened faces I see James, a head and a half taller than the Afghans. I am relieved he is there, but do my best to act nonchalant. He looks different from when I met him in London and managed to talk myself into coming on this trip. His Western-style anorak covers a typical Afghan *tumbaan*, a long cream-coloured shirt that reaches mid-thigh over matching baggy trousers, while a large, grey chequered scarf is wrapped around his shoulders. His dark, curly hair has taken on a suitably wild look and a thick beard now covers what were once clean-shaven features.

'Welcome to Afghanistan!' he beams and shakes my hand.

A driver in a silver Hiace people carrier is waiting for us. His friendly grin immediately betrays the tough living conditions here and the patchy level of medical services. Once more, I realise how fortunate I am to live where I do. James introduces the thin-faced young man as Aasif. He slips out from behind the steering wheel and slides open the side door with a grubby hand that looks transplanted from someone twice his age. I avert my eyes from the yellowing fingernails and smile a hello. He, too, is wearing a two-piece *tumbaan*, but his is black and, I suspect, part of a very limited wardrobe, not a decorative add-on. He heaves my bag into the van and I climb in the back after it. The door slams shut, he and James get in the front, and off we go.

For a while, we drive along a wide, tree-lined avenue, but are soon in the chaos of the city's mud-spattered traffic, holding tight as we drop into potholes filled with melt water from the recent snowfall James tells me they have had. Seemingly keen to make conversation, he asks if my journey was OK and if I am tired. I hardly slept on the overnight flight from Istanbul, but I am wide awake and eager to see as much as possible: I have not come here to sleep. We swerve to avoid a battered lorry that suddenly pulls out, coughing thick black smoke from its exhaust as the engine growls. Our driver blasts away on the horn, curses in Dari, the dialect of Farsi spoken here, and then looks at us and laughs. The truck is crammed full with chickens, their white feathers sticking through its panelled sides. It spews out another filthy cloud of fumes as if answering back.

'First stop is the guesthouse,' explains James, as the traffic slows to a halt.

Here and there, black, red and green tricolours hang from flagpoles of government buildings where once the white flag of the Taliban flew. At a large roundabout, three huge armoured personnel carriers roar past, horns blasting, the Afghan soldiers sitting on top of them anonymous behind black sunglasses. We trundle on, going by a newly renovated but uninspiring mosque on a corner, and then we are driving past ugly office buildings from the 1970s and 80s, or perhaps they are hospitals or hotels. It is impossible to tell: their dirty windows reveal nothing.

I peer out of the side of the van at the concrete blast walls that surround all sensitive buildings, rolls of razor wire along their top.

Afghan soldiers, dressed up in modern military attire, pace slowly back and forth. I ask James if things are getting any better, if he has noticed any improvements during the years he has been bringing tourists here with his adventure travel company. He hesitates before replying. I wonder if he is gathering his thoughts or merely contemplating which answer to give.

'Yes,' he says finally, turning to face me, his grey eyes looking straight into mine, 'things are slowly picking up. But Afghan society is very different from what we are used to in the West,' he adds, saying he thinks it will be a long time before democracy as we know it takes root in the culture. I see Aasif looking at me in the rear view mirror and glance at James. 'The driver doesn't speak English,' he tells me with a disarming smile.

I ask what a 'jammer' is and tell him about the puzzling sign I saw at the airport. James grins and tells me it is a device for blocking the radio waves, usually from mobile phones, used to detonate IEDs. 'Improvised Explosive Devices,' he winks, seeing the blank look on my face.

We inch forward along a one-way street lined with bare trees. I wonder if they are dead or if it is the winter that has reduced them to skeletons. We crawl past shop fronts with displays of shiny Western-style suits, halt in front of a sports store with tailors' dummies dressed in the blue and yellow national baseball strip, and trundle by windows full of brightly coloured dresses, their tight satin bodices giving way to ruched folds of fabric that reach to the floor as large vivid triangles. We continue slowly along the congested road with its eclectic mix of fashion stores; such is the main shopping thoroughfare in the country's capital. The fairytale gowns on show tell of a different life behind closed doors, in safety, but here on the street, there are few women and most of those I see are covered in traditional *chadris*, the azure, or occasionally black, *burqas* that cover them from head to foot, with just a small mesh for the wearer to peer through. I reflect on the striking contrast to the stylish modern clothes worn by the young woman who gave me my visa in the Afghan embassy back home, although even she half-heartedly draped a black scarf over the back of her head as I entered the cramped office she shared with a colleague. We speed up a bit. Now we are driving past something equating to a park: through the railings I can see compacted earth, plastic seating and more bare trees. Some men are milling about in small groups, others sit around. Perhaps in summer families come here.

We turn into a narrow side road, coffee-coloured snow piled in heaps along its sides. The van plunges into puddles that must be ankle deep and bounces out the other side with a burst of revs. We stop at a corner and James announces we have arrived. Aasif leaps out and slides the van door open. Clambering out carefully, I try to avoid the worst of the mud. James pushes a button next to a battered metal doorway at the corner of a high wall, triggering electronic birdcall somewhere way beyond the other side. While we wait, Aasif unloads my bag and staggers towards us. After blowing into his hands to warm them, James rings the bell again and once more there is the distant chirping noise. A bolt slides, a key turns and the door swings open to reveal a young man in regulation baggy clothing. A warm, genuine smile extends across his tanned face as he and James exchange greetings in Dari. I nod and say hello to our host whom my compatriot introduces as Faisal. Little clouds of vapour float between us as our breath chills in the morning air. I am fascinated by his blue eyes, feeling as if I alone have found evidence to finally support the long-held belief that the people here still carry genes left behind by Alexander the Great's soldiers. Faisal looks at me, apparently puzzled by my interest, his eyes sparkling as if on cue. He locks up behind us while James and I make our way along the concrete path that cuts diagonally across the humble garden. My guide explains he finds the low-key approach safest: we are better off here in a modest bed and breakfast frequented by Afghans than in a luxury hotel targeted by the Taliban. I look at the scraggy rose bushes that are dotted round the edge of the grass, intermingled with plastic flowers. A few foil windmills on sticks, the sort one would more expect to see at the seaside, stand here and there, colourful but motionless. The guesthouse is simple: I think it must once have been a private home. The path continues alongside it, leading to the main entrance in front of which stands a rusting, Soviet-era piece of machinery on wheels. It could be some sort of miniature tractor; it looks as if it has been there for years. We take off our shoes before entering the building, leaving them next to a pile of men's dusty black slip-ons and trainers with flattened backstays. Faisal catches us up, grinning as he kicks his shoes off before he squeezes past and disappears inside.

I hoist my bag up the step and over the threshold into the hallway, wondering if, just once, I should try travelling light. An ageing computer, deeper than it is wide, with a sticky-looking keyboard stands lifeless on a Formica table. I follow James to a ground-floor room, wheeling my luggage across the thin, red pile of the traditionally patterned carpet. He flicks a switch and a dim economy bulb begins to glow, gradually illuminating the room. Three single beds with headboards and footboards in dark wood are arranged in a U shape, each with a single pillow and several layers of rough blankets. Points of daylight fight their way through the purple lace curtains that cover the windows. I can choose any one of the beds, says James, handing me a large bottle of water, which he seems to have conjured up from nowhere. Once I have parked my duffel bag next to the low glass table that stands between the divans, there is hardly any floor space left. We sit down on the slightly concave beds facing each other and James picks up a flimsy blue plastic bag out of which he produces an off-white *tumbaan* and a choice of three scarves.

'It's not a question of going around in disguise,' he reassures me, 'just a matter of reducing visibility.'

I point out that my polar anorak is bright orange, but he assures me it is not a problem. I pull the baggy outfit over my jeans and thick pullover, put my coat back on and then wrap a polyester scarf, the blue and gold chequered one, round my shoulders.

Feeling like the Michelin man, I emerge with James on to the street. I half waddle, half pick my way along the broken pavement, trying to avoid twisting an ankle or losing a foot into the depths of sodden earth that lie between slabs of concrete. The street is lined with parked Japanese cars caked with dried mud. I tell James I think Kabul is the muddiest place I have ever visited. He laughs, saying it hardly ever rains in Afghanistan: nearly all the country's water comes from melted snow. We walk past brightly lit stores, each little more than a single room. Mobile phones, groceries, CDs and T-shirts: each shop has found its niche. A little further on, we pass a row of florists where the few real specimens are greatly outnumbered by flamboyant displays of artificial blooms in colours that Mother Nature would be embarrassed to unleash. Apart from the fact that most of the people shopping, talking or otherwise going about their business are men, everything appears surprisingly normal. As we cross a busy road, I am grateful that the traffic is so bad that we are able to wend our way between the crawling vehicles without risking life and limb.

'We're going to Chicken Street,' says James.

I brace myself for a grisly food market-cum-abattoir, but instead find the place full of shops selling jewellery, antiques, carpets and traditional Afghan clothing. Half-derelict buildings from the latter years of the twentieth century stand next to two-storey constructions of indeterminable age, ugly panels of reflective glass alongside shop windows with pull-down metal blinds.

'Chicken Street has been a big attraction for tourists to Kabul since the days when the country was on the Hippy Trail,' James tells me, as we pause to look in a shop window. Mineral rocks, some sliced and polished to reveal concentric patterns, line the shelves alongside all manner of items made of lapis lazuli, the semi-precious stone prized since antiquity for its intense blue colour.

'It comes from the north-eastern province of Badakhshan,' says James, his hands in his anorak pockets. 'The Sar-i Sang mines there have been worked for over six thousand years; they were the main source of lapis lazuli for the Ancient World. Even that found in the artefacts from Tutankhamun's tomb and the royal treasures of Ur came from Afghanistan.'

I look at the penholders, paper-weights and carved animals set out on the glass shelves and, perhaps unfairly, compare their unappealing designs to the wonders of Ancient Egypt and Mesopotamia. As for Badakhshan, I have never heard of it: the only place that makes the news back home is Helmand Province and for all the wrong reasons. The two men in the shop see us peering at the display and, smiling, beckon us to come inside. When they see our hesitation, they quickly appear at the door grinning and fire off a volley of questions in excellent English, asking how we are, where we are from and what we would like to buy today. My heart almost stops as I hear James tell them we are British but, to my surprise, their reaction is friendly.

'Welcome to Afghanistan!' they chime, almost in unison. Like everyone I see here, their tanned faces look weathered, a result, I imagine, of the bitter-cold winters and hot, dry summers. They are keen on a sale and the older one with the thick moustache assures us he has beautiful gifts we could buy for our families, vowing solemnly to make us a special price. We smile our excuses, say we might come back later and continue on our way.

A shop selling waistcoats, jackets and hats catches my attention. I am tempted by the piles of *karakuls*, the typical Kabul caps made from curly Astrakhan fur, and the heaps of traditional *pakuls,* a sort of woollen beret in earthy colours: either one would make an exotic addition to my hat collection. But, when we go in, I am dismayed to see the place is full of fur coats, aimed, no doubt, at well-paid expats working here. The hook-nosed owner, a man of indeterminable age with greasy hair, emerges from a recess, black eyes flashing. Are we looking for hats? Or perhaps a nice leather jacket? he grimaces, whisking a cheap-looking black three-quarter-length coat off one of the crowded rails and thrusting it at us. Put off by the snarling fox pelts dangling everywhere and the unpleasant, musty smell, I say I am just browsing and make for the open door.

'Perhaps a nice waistcoat?' he calls after us, but we are already back outside.

I ask James why it is called Chicken Street, as we saunter past a huge hole between two houses. Foundations have been laid for a new building, but the site is empty. He says it is because many years ago there was indeed a poultry market, only later being replaced by the sort of shops we see around us today. Walking along the road, we are greeted by smiles and the occasional 'Hello!' from storekeepers standing in doorways. We stop in front of one shop selling carpets, not the traditional patterns one might expect, but rugs with images of tanks, machine guns and fighter planes woven into them. I try to decide if they are a tasteless gimmick aimed at foreigners or a contemporary version of the genuine article, adapted to reflect life as experienced by people here. I wonder whether I should buy one, the novelty of the strange item starting to appeal. Perhaps it is the altitude.

James suggests we go to the international bookshop, famous for featuring in the controversial tale *The Bookseller of Kabul* in which the Norwegian journalist Åsne Seierstad recounted her stay with the owner and his family, a depiction which he strongly contested. I can buy my stamps and postcards there, James tells me. We make our way along the high pavement, passing stores selling paper, soft drinks or haircuts, until we arrive at a makeshift roundabout where a policeman is half-heartedly attempting to control the erratic traffic. Red and white barricades stand randomly in the middle of the roads leading to the junction. We wait for a gap between the cars before dashing across the street to the green-fronted store. Inside, it is as quiet and library-like as bookshops the world over. Near the entrance, its walls are lined from floor to ceiling with an amazing selection of publications, mostly about Afghanistan and the region, but in the farther corners of the labyrinthine shop there are children's editions, foreign-language dictionaries, course books and encyclopaedias. I ponder my baggage allowance for the return flight before starting to select a handful of postcards from the wacky collection that fills the racks. Next to photographs of magnificent scenery and historical buildings, palaces and mosques are pictures of bearded Afghans cheerfully brandishing semi-automatic weapons. Looking at a lurid image of the twelfth-century Minaret of Jam in the Ghor Province, I realise I am unfamiliar with most of the places featured on the cards and feel ashamed that I have arrived in Afghanistan knowing so little about the country's architectural riches. I reflect glumly on the cycle of violence and poverty, and how the security situation chokes off the development of tourism, an industry that could do so much to help improve the lives of people here.

I take my selection of postcards to the man sitting behind the counter. He is filling out what looks like an old-fashioned ledger. In his late thirties, I wonder if he is the Sultan Khan character featured in the book, but think better of it than to ask. I have never read the work and, for all I know, the protagonist might be eighty years old. With his Western-style shirt and trousers and absence of any form of scarf or turban, the clean-shaven man in front of me looks like any mature student from the Middle East one might see in London. I enquire after stamps and am surprised to be given a handful of specimens dating from years ago. They are still valid, the man earnestly assures me through his thick-rimmed glasses as if reading my mind while I study a stamp commemorating the 1984 Winter Olympics in Sarajevo. Picking up another, I am surprised to see the words '*Postes afghanes*' in French. A faint smile brightening up his face, the seemingly telepathic bookseller tells me it is because the former king was a Francophile. I wonder which one he means: the last monarch, Mohammed Zahir Shar, was, in 1973, ousted in a coup, a fate he shared with three of his four predecessors. I return to browsing the shelves where tales of *Boys Own*-style nineteenth-century battles are interspersed with reviews of the political situation and studies on the role of Islam in the region. I could spend hours in the place: it is crammed full with books one would never come across in a shop at home.

But we must go, says James with a friendly smile, if I want to visit the bird market, the last remaining authentic bazaar in Kabul. I have accumulated a handful of books, but decide to buy just one, a volume entitled *Afghanistan Over a Cup of Tea* penned by the ageing American Nancy Hatch Dupree, an expert on the history, art and archaeology of the country who has lived here on and off for decades. The text on the back says that each of the forty-eight chronicles can be read in about the time it takes to drink a cup of hot *chai*. As I finish handing over my *Afghanis* to pay, James is already hovering near the door. He bundles me out of the shop while ringing his local partner. The call over, he explains that the bird market is less safe than other parts of the city and that the visit will have to be brief.

We make our way back to the guesthouse where Taimur, James's business associate, and the driver are waiting for us. Clad in a 1950s-style leather flying jacket and a black *tumbaan*, the surprisingly long-haired man introduces himself in grammatically perfect English with the sort of refined Pakistani accent that makes me think of Benazir Bhutto. In countries where life is hard, looks can be deceptive, but I reckon Taimur, like James, is about thirty. He says we should get going. We pile into the van and are once again back in the city's traffic, now gridlocked in one-way streets, moments later free-flowing along wide roads. We trundle over a bridge that spans the narrow Kabul River, its shallow, foaming waters streaming past all manner of rubbish on the riverbed in the way I imagine many urban rivers in Europe used to until comparatively recently. Languishing somewhere at the bottom of the World Bank's development list of 180 countries, Afghanistan is the poorest place I have visited, but, even so, I find myself surprised, not just by the deprivation, but by the lack of development. In India, too, I saw grinding poverty, but it existed cheek-by-jowl with signs of great wealth, both past and present. Here, as we drive through Kabul, all I see are dilapidated buildings, garbage and what looks like a medieval society dumped, bewildered, into an alien world. There are glimpses of modernity, but they look as if they will leave with the troops when they finally go, or otherwise quickly succumb to whatever follows the withdrawal.

'Where has all the aid money gone?' I ask.

Taimur says some has gone on reconstruction and on improving roads, such as the one to Bamyan in the centre of the country, but a lot has simply disappeared.

'You know, my friend, Afghan society is very different to that in the West,' he adds, turning to face me from his seat in the front of the van and echoing James's words with a slight lecturing tone. 'You can't expect everything to function here like in your country.'

'What do you think will happen when the international troops pull out?' I venture, deciding to change the subject.

Looking again at the road ahead, Taimur utters a short, cold laugh. I cannot decide whether it is of resignation or because he considers my question naïve. His gaze still fixed at some point beyond the windscreen, he says the Taliban will be back in power within a fortnight. James is more optimistic: he thinks enough people will be reluctant to see a return to the sort of regime they had before to prevent that scenario. They make light of their diverging views, as if the discussion is one they have aired many times before. They agree to differ and we drop the subject.

A short while later, our silver van pulls up amidst a chaotic mass of vehicles, some parked, others with their engines running. Ostensibly, we are at the side of a road, but it looks more like a yawning gap between two rows of crumbling buildings separated by a hotchpotch of lorries, cars and carts. Crowds mill about in front of hole-in-the-wall shops above which colourful hoardings advertise everything from mobile phone services to baby food. Hawkers wander around, some limping, as they try to sell pens, paper handkerchiefs and little bags of nuts, wizened hands proffering cheap goods while weary faces silently tell of souls that have tired of life. Taimur appears nervous: since the end of the discussion about the country's future, he has made half a dozen phone calls, the subject of which I could only guess from the intonation and, whenever he looked at the driver, from the expression on his face. He tells James to wait in the van and then, turning to me, says we will only be able to make a quick tour of the bird market, known locally as the Ka Farushi bazaar. I slide open the door and slip out into the noisy, messy world of the shopping street, meeting Taimur in front of the vehicle. He stomps off towards a gap in the buildings where a narrow lane, the Alley of the Straw Sellers, the strangely-named home to the bird market, begins. I walk briskly after the stocky figure, doing my best to keep up and feeling very conspicuous in my bright orange parka, despite my *tumbaan* and voluminous scarf. We dash through the bazaar, my attempts to linger and look at the doves, canaries and finches that fill the stacks of cages being curtailed by Taimur's constant exhortations to hurry up. Among the cooing and chirping that fills the air, I think I recognise the sound of a nightingale's whistle, but there is no time to investigate: I do not want to lose sight of my guide among the stallholders and shoppers. Scurrying along, now and then I catch a faint whiff of avian odours, but the cold air does much to suppress what in the heat of summer must surely be more pungent smells.

'These are *kowks*,' explains Taimur, suddenly stopping in front of a row of domed wicker cages containing plump birds with red legs and feet. 'They are a *special* type of partridge,' he says, his eyes widening. 'We once had this British man who came on one of our trips. He knew everything about birds and he told me they are Chukars.' As he says this, Taimur's chest seems to swell like those of the birds themselves. With their grey and buff plumage, black collars and coral-red beaks, they look very much like the red-legged partridges found in Europe. Squatting in their cages, they seem content with their life of captivity and I wonder if they would know what to do if they were ever released.

'And people eat these?' I ask.

'No! The *kowks* are used for fighting! It is a very popular sport here: men are gambling a lot of money on them. On Fridays, they take the birds to the park and make them fight.' Taimur studies me for a moment and then turns and marches off.

As I follow him, I am vaguely aware of bearded men in traditional dress and coats, dark eyes watching us from beneath white turban caps and mushroom-coloured *pakuls* as we hurriedly make our way through the cluttered street. Everything seems brown or beige, the buildings, the mud, the woodwork, even the smiles. After we have scuttled our way for a few more minutes, as if finally having satisfied a child's misplaced curiosity, Taimur tells me that we have seen all there is to see and that we should turn back. I am disappointed: I had expected a visit to the ancient market to be one of the cultural highlights in Kabul with the opportunity to meander and browse. Instead, I have seen nothing more than a blur and have scarcely had time to absorb my surroundings. I get no sense of hostility or danger and wonder if Taimur is not overplaying the situation. But I am unfamiliar with the society and its ways. I know I might not pick up on signals of which he is astutely aware: my safety is in his hands and I have no choice but to scurry after him, suppressing my irritation. As we climb back into the Hiace, James asks cheerfully how it was.

'Quick,' I huff, and try to smile.

As Aasif launches the little van into the mix of traffic, carts, and people, James says we will go to look at the old city walls. It is a short drive past crumbling buildings and stacks of timber, slender tree trunks lying next to planks of varying lengths and widths. I reflect on what I have seen so far and am struck by how normal, at least for a poor developing country, much of the city seems: daily life carries on. People are working, talking, plying their trades: nobody is rioting, stamping on flags or burning effigies. It is very different from the impression of Afghanistan I had formed before coming here. From out of the van window, I look up to see the fortifications snaking their way down the edge of a steep hill at the bottom of which the brown Kabul River flows. Tiny, flat-roofed houses cling to the hillside, looking more like make-do shelters than homes. I wonder how they can possibly afford protection from the severe Afghan winter: I can think of ski resorts in Europe at a lower altitude. My modest guesthouse starts to look cosy and inviting in comparison. We do not stop, but instead carry on through the bustling city towards the royal residence of Darul Aman. James is not sure whether we will be able to go in or not.

The derelict palace stands on a small rise in the middle of barren ground some sixteen kilometres from the city centre. Remaining patches of snow brighten up the otherwise drab surroundings of muddy earth and stick trees, the scene evoking the landscapes depicted in depressing paintings of First World War battlefields. At the base of the driveway leading up to the main entrance, we pass a large billboard with a photograph of two boys bearing weapons. Over their image a large diagonal cross is 'daubed' in blood red as part of the poster. I cannot read the script, but Taimur confirms it is part of a campaign against child soldiers. At the top of the ramp we pull up and clamber out of the van. Only now do I notice an airship floating some distance away above the city, its silvery skin catching the sunlight. It is moored by a long cable that descends to earth like an umbilical cord before disappearing behind a cluster of buildings. Taimur says it is for aerial reconnaissance with its cameras watching what is happening on the ground. I am unsure whether to believe him, although, here, anything could be possible.

A couple of soldiers stand guard in front of the improvised fence of rolls of barbed and razor wire. They pick up their guns and walk towards us, the jackets of their green and brown uniforms open, revealing khaki T-shirts beneath. With his round face, green eyes and curly hair, the younger of the two looks very different to other Afghans I have seen. His somewhat thickset colleague sports a khaki *kepi* on his head and looks us up and down suspiciously. The two men seem impervious to the cold, which I find mercilessly pervades the multiple layers of clothing I am wearing. Taimur greets the soldiers and, after an increasingly jolly exchange, they part the spaghetti-like mix of steel wire and, like doormen at a plush hotel, smilingly wave us through.

Built in the 1920s, the 150-room, neo-classical building could be anywhere in Europe, perhaps Berlin in 1945: it was shelled by the Mujahadeen after the Soviets left and its walls are pockmarked with bullet holes. The metal girders that mark the outline of what was once the roof remind me of the Atomic Bomb Dome in

Hiroshima. We make our way inside, picking our way over rubble, avoiding puddles and passing piles of plasterwork that has given up trying to cover the brick walls. We head up a curved concrete staircase without a banister to the first floor where icicles are dangling from the roof. A gaping hole the size of a car in the floor of the main corridor is surrounded by rubble and looks as if it could expand at any moment to wrench the ground from beneath us. I look out from a gap in the wall at a large, low building directly opposite a few hundred metres away.

'It's the new parliament, ' says James.

Still under construction, like the palace, it is an empty shell. I wonder if it will one day be completed or if these two buildings will forever remain testimonials to failures of governance in this country riven by tribal and ethnic rivalries. Beyond the symmetrical architecture of the would-be legislature with its pointed, arched windows lie the snow-covered mountains of the Hindu Kush, their imposing beauty in stark contrast to the drabness and poverty of the rapidly growing Afghan capital, their serenity a foil to the underlying fear of violence that hangs in the city like an invisible gas.

We continue up to the top floor. An icy wind blows through the corridors where graffiti scribbled by Russian soldiers, complete with dates from the early 1980s, still marks the candy-pink and peach plasterwork. We enter what must once have been an elegant room with a view across the city. Now, it is mostly bare brickwork and open to the sky, a concave network of rusting iron hanging precariously above our heads. We crunch our way across the thin layer of snow to the half dozen or so arched windows and look out on the low-rise metropolis of four million. The hum of distant traffic, punctuated by car horns, drifts over the rooftops. I contemplate the urban sprawl that covers the valley floor and consider how it compares to the Kabul of the era when the British East India Company army under Elphinstone made its disastrous retreat in 1842. Of the 4,500 troops who tried to reach the British garrison in Jalalabad, only one officer survived. The rest, along with some 12,000 civilians and camp followers, fell at the hands of Afghan forces led by Akbar Khan, the country's Emir for just three years. Afghanistan, it seems, is a country nobody can subjugate. Even Alexander the Great, who founded numerous towns here, including Herat, Bagram and Kandahar, was unable to bring the fierce tribes under lasting control. Over the course of the last two hundred years, the British, the Soviets, the Americans and the British, again, have tried to hold sway over these tough people, seemingly unable to learn from past mistakes or the experience of others. I try to make sense of the mismatch between the reputation Afghans have for merciless ferocity when defending their country with the friendliness I have encountered so far.

James says we should be on our way, bringing me out of my daydream and making me suddenly aware of the cold wind blowing in my face. I take a couple of pictures, framed by what were once windows, before turning to follow James and Taimur back through the palace. As we make our way carefully down the stairs, I ask myself what Amanullah Khan, the country's modernising king who had the place erected during his ten-year reign, would think if he could see it today. And I wonder what my own house, built some four decades before this royal abode, will look like eighty years hence. Or if it will even be still standing.

Back outside, the guards are keen to know if we enjoyed the visit and willingly pose for photographs in front of the rolls of defensive wire, guns in their hands, broad smiles on their faces. We thank them and head back to the van where Aasif is listening to local music on the radio. We roll back down the raised driveway, the resilience of our tinny vehicle never ceasing to amaze me as we bounce in and out of yet more potholes. Taking a swig from a bottle of water, James says we still have time to go to the Nadir Shah hill to see the kite-flying. He asks if I have read the novel *The Kite Runner*; I am ashamed to admit that I have not. We make our way through the city's chaotic traffic, a mixture of small Asian cars filled with Afghans and Toyota Land Cruisers chauffeuring expats, who, I imagine, work for NGOs or donor country development agencies and are on the way to their next important meeting. Occasionally, a Hummer ploughs past, its loud horn impatiently demanding that the slow-moving mass of vehicles let it through.

Eventually, we leave the muddy urban streets and join a line of traffic climbing a road lined by grassy embankments and a few trees with vestiges of green. It seems almost bucolic in comparison to the turmoil of the city. Soon, we are at the top of the hill where crowds are wandering past a handful of roadside stalls selling drinks and nuts. Aasif drops us off and then parks up a little further on. The greenery of the ascent has given way to an arid hilltop where boys and men are busy flying kites of various shapes and sizes. A constant fluttering fills the air as the paper and bamboo kites soar and dive. I duck to avoid a purple and orange shape that swoops towards me, a shiver running down my spine as it brushes past my head with a gush of cold air before climbing skywards again. I look up, trying to see where it has gone, but it is lost among the colourful quadrilaterals that are hovering and diving like origami seagulls. Others are so high I can hardly see them. I am amazed: as a child, I struggled to get my kite even to leave the ground, a frustration that quickly killed my interest in the whole exercise.

Taimur tells me *gudiparan bazi*, or kite-flying, is very popular in Afghanistan. *Gudiparan* means 'flying doll', he smiles, explaining that operating each kite requires two people: the leader who actually flies it and the second person who holds the *charkha*, a wooden drum on a stick around which the wire is wrapped. As our eyes follow the paper shapes darting about the sky above us, he describes how the strings, or *tars*, are covered with tiny bits of glass glued in place, the aim being to try to sever the cord of the other kites. We watch for a while until I am distracted by a man galloping towards us on a palomino horse. It is tetchy and resists his attempts to keep it under control, even though he is clearly an accomplished rider, finally managing to bring it to a halt a short distance away. The snorting beast paces backwards on the hard ground while the man pulls tightly on the reins. It looks as if it is performing a dance. I wonder if it can see the ruts that are chiselled into the compacted earth and if it is the kites that are making it nervous: at home, even a flapping bag is enough to strike fear into the equine heart. As I watch the man sitting astride colourful blankets, his legs gripping the agitated animal, my thoughts turn to the horsemen of central Asia who, under Genghis Khan and others, used battle techniques based on their mastery of these animals to conquer vast swathes of Eurasia. Surrounding their foe, they rode round and round whilst constantly attacking, picking them off one by one until victory was theirs. For no obvious reason, the man suddenly gains full control of the horse and steers it in a calm trot across the flat hill, weaving a way between the kite flyers.

'Under the Taliban, kite-flying was banned,' sighs James, as a group of youngsters dash past on their way to claim one that has been cut down in battle. My attention is once again focused on the *gudiparan bazi*. 'They considered it un-Islamic,' he tells me.

We wander over to a stall where a couple of men in *tumbaans* and suit jackets are selling kites and string. A throng of boys watches intently as a couple of lanky teenagers choose a kite; its turquoise-blue colour reminds me of the domes of the mosques I saw in neighbouring Uzbekistan the year before. Despite the competition between the kite flyers, the atmosphere is jovial, almost festive. The two slim youths walk off a short distance with their *gudiparan* and *charkha* and, after a few minutes' laughing and arguing while they tie them together, are finally ready to launch their new acquisition.

The taller of the pair takes charge of the kite, leaving his apparently younger companion to hold the large bobbin. He lifts up the *gudiparan*, waiting for a gust of wind, the thinness of his arms obvious in his ribbed burgundy pullover which has risen up to expose his midriff to the chilly air. He talks excitedly to his friend, but his gaze is fixed on the kite. As if fulfilling a wish granted by some invisible genie, a blast of cold wind from far across the Hindu Kush arrives on our hill top. The boy throws the kite into the air and we watch as it soars upwards into the wide sky. Like a bird released from a cage, it flutters freely, dropping for a heart-stopping moment before again gracefully making its way aloft. I look at the two youths: their entire concentration is on the *gudiparan*, the elder of the two giving instructions to his friend with the *charkha*, a sense of urgency in his voice. Now, others around us are raising their eyes to the sky to follow the kite's progress. A small boy pulls excitedly at his father's jacket sleeve while the kite vendors take a break from chatting to their customers to watch their fragile creation weave its way through the sharp spring air. I look around me: all eyes are on the blue kite. Suddenly, a murmuring begins, turning quickly to shouting. Hands point skyward. I look up to see a plain white *gudiparan* flying below the one belonging to the two adolescents. It darts back and forth, up and down, before quickly encircling the *tar* of their kite and closing in. It is all over in an instant: to gasps from those around us, the string is cut. The two youths cry out as their kite flies free for a second and then hovers before plummeting towards the ground as the wind suddenly drops. A band of small boys charges off in the direction of the falling paper-covered frame, followed a moment later by the two shouting teenagers. James and Taimur watch the scene, hands in their jacket pockets, heads tucked deep into their thick collars. I open my mouth to speak, but nothing comes out. Instead, I find myself tasting cold air. The two kite sellers are once again busying themselves with potential customers, interest in the blue *gudiparan* has dropped as quickly as the wind, and the crowd has melted away. I try to see who is flying the white kite, but, when I look up again, it is nowhere to be seen. Now, only a few *gudiparans* float, almost hesitantly, in the bright sky above and, in the distance, motionless, is the silver airship.

Dreams of Rain

Barren, brown, dry: an inhospitable landscape of the sort that appears in science-fiction films rose before us, its jagged mountains uninviting and hinting at danger. Only the parallel lines crossing the sedimentary rock at a steep angle told of other epochs millions of years ago when, in their youth, these giants lay beneath the sea. Now rugged masses, they stood lifeless, yet still exuded a strange majesty and beauty. Ahead, a square, flat-roofed building roughly garnished with thorn scrub told us we were nearing the point to turn off. Approaching the V-junction, we saw two old Mercedes parked at the side of the road, three bearded men and a few children standing around them. As we slowed down, the men, one much older than the other two, began waving. Unsure as to their motives, we smiled weakly and gave a single, cursory wave as we drove past and headed on to the dirt track, leaving the smooth tarmac of the main road and an ephemeral veil of dust behind us.

The route began to climb, the rough way quickly turning into a rocky and potholed ascent with hairpin bends. Frédéric wrestled with the steering wheel as it pulled this way and that. We lurched to the right and I banged my head on the window, despite being strapped into my seat.

'Sorry,' said Frédéric absently, as we bounced around.

My French friend had asked me if I wanted to join him on a trip to Oman and Dubai over the Easter break, an invitation I had accepted without hesitation. Now, with my head aching, I wondered how I could so easily have forgotten his rather particular driving style. I held on tight as the 4x4 dipped and rolled on the bumpy road, its engine revving gruffly. Soon, between the gaps in the rocky embankment at the road's edge we began to get glimpses of the parched valley below; sometimes there was nothing at all separating us and stomach-churning drops into the abyss. As we turned a corner, we were suddenly confronted by two young boys at the roadside, one slightly taller than the other, large bags on their backs. They stepped aside to let us by, our Land Cruiser reducing its voice to a low growl as we rumbled past. They waved, small hands at the end of slender arms, and grinned broken smiles. We continued a little further. And then we stopped. Frédéric yanked the handbrake on and I opened the car door.

'*Merhaba!* Do you want a lift?' I called back.

They appeared to understand and came scampering to the vehicle. In an instant they had clambered inside and were giggling with excitement as we set off up the steep hill. They wiggled and danced to the Arabic music on the radio and told us of their favourite songs, they laughed at their own jokes and asked us where we were from. At least that is what I imagined they were saying: in fact, we understood nothing other than that they were called Ali and Sayyid. And, in a similar vein, I do not think they grasped much of what we said, except when, tapping our chests, we told them our names. They kept repeating them, laughing when they realised they could not pronounce the words properly, but showing a keenness to learn by trying again and again. They seemed impressed by the smart interior of the vehicle, big brown eyes sparkling with the fun of the unexpected adventure as they explored the seatback pockets and moved the central armrest up and down.

As the Land Cruiser dropped a gear, I imagined its mechanical roar reverberating across the valley, where the calls of wild animals could once be heard. Frédéric knows I think he always drives one gear lower than necessary, but I have given up passing comment: I sense he likes the noise the extra revs make. The road, such as it was, became even steeper, the occasional feathery, wild almond tree providing a welcome touch of green. My thoughts turned to the soldiers who would have worked in the searing heat to dig and shovel the switchback up the seemingly endless climb through the Hajar Mountains and of the pittance they would have been handed at the end of their labours. But, rather selfishly, I was grateful that their toil meant we could explore the remote Omani enclave of Musandam with relative ease. Ali pulled something out of his bag. It was a school book, battered round the edges. He tried to lean forward to show it to us, but we had made them fasten their seatbelts before setting off. Only now did we realise why the men standing next to the two Mercedes had been waving: they had wanted us to take the children along as we headed up the road towards Jebel al Harim – the Mountain of Women. I remembered reading that many of the pupils attending the school in Musandam's diminutive capital Khasab live so far away that they spend the entire week there only returning to their families at the weekend. The two boys we had picked up had been on the long march home; the others we had passed, giving them nothing more than a suspicious wave, had not been so lucky.

We turned a corner and were surprised to be confronted by a lush meadow no bigger than a bowling green. Beyond it was a simple concrete house and a short washing line from which a few T-shirts hung limply in the heat. We slowed down to drop the boys off, but they bombarded us with cries of '*La! La!*', Arabic for no, and waved enthusiastically for us to continue. We carried on, passing half a dozen similar farmsteads, each with a square tank outside to which the government delivers water to supplement that from the winter rains stored in the traditional cisterns or *birka*. Eventually, we arrived at a broad, single-storey building. It stood surrounded by dry stone walls and grass, together with a couple of wizened trees under the patchy shade of which a donkey, not much bigger than a large dog, stood tethered, motionless. Ali and Sayyid began shouting and un-clicked their seatbelts. We pulled up and they jumped out, calling '*Shukran!*' as they skipped away, their bulging bags on their shoulders. We waved goodbye and continued across the Sayh Plateau, a fleeting oasis of green alfalfa and wheat, and a few small palm trees and donkeys amidst the brown, grey and mustard-coloured mountains. We wondered how long the walk would have taken the boys if we had not given them a lift and felt bad about the other children we had driven past. As we carried on towards Jebel al Harim, at over 2,000 metres the highest peak on the peninsula, I contemplated the lengths to which our two passengers and others like them in this impoverished part of the Sultanate went to get an education. When Oman's current ruler, Sultan Qaboos bin Said, came to the throne in 1970 the country had only one school. In the course of his reign, he has built countless more as part of the celebrated 'Renaissance' and modernisation of the realm, but Ali and Sayyid still had to trek up and down the mountain every week. I compared the boys' situation to that of their peers back in Europe who often seem ignorant of their good fortune and are ferried the short distance back and forth to school like little princes and princesses. I wondered what sort of schooling Ali and Sayyid would get and how long they would be able to continue studying until economic pressure perhaps forced them to go to work if, indeed, there was any to be had in this isolated corner of Arabia.

Our Land Cruiser took us ever higher along the Jabal Sayh Road, the quality of which suddenly improved, potholes giving way to smooth dust. The emptiness of the rock-strewn landscape around us reminded me that, for all its burgeoning population of seven billion, vast tracts of this globe are empty and virtually devoid of human habitation. We skirted Jebel al Harim and, after following the zigzag road a couple of kilometres further, stopped and got out to admire the view. I took a few photographs of the mountains and a couple with Frédéric in the foreground, smiling, his hands in the pockets of his perfectly pressed trousers. I am always amazed by people who are able to strike a pose and suddenly light up their faces with a convincing grin as easily as flicking a switch. As Frédéric wandered off a short distance, I retreated to a large rock and contemplated the panorama that extended before us, rugged rocks side by side with pillow-shaped folds. Above, a lone raptor circled slowly on the thermals. Here, silence, a rare commodity at home, surrounded us so completely that after a few minutes I was convinced I could even hear my own pulse. It would be difficult to think of a greater contrast with the glittering, noisy metropolis of Dubai in the United Arab Emirates – the UAE – from where I had driven us the day before: the hi-tech oasis of wealth and luxury at the edge of the Arabian desert might as well have been on another world. The desolate scene in front of us, now a palette of terracotta, russet and cinnamon and looking as if it had been sculpted with a knife, could be Mars, I thought, but then, with no sense of disappointment, remembered that mountains on the Red Planet dwarf those on Earth. The sun burning the nape of my neck, my binoculars scanned the landscape for a glimpse of a Tahr, a sort of stocky mountain goat that lives in these parts. The optimist in me hoped I might even see an Arabian leopard – a profile on a distant outcrop perhaps, or a spotted form slinking through the valley below – but I knew the chances of seeing one were very remote. Hope is the greatest incentive, but, after staring through the lenses for some time, I realised I would have to content myself with simply knowing that there might be one out there in the barren wilderness, perhaps sleeping in a cave, maybe silently watching from afar.

The next day, back in Khasab, we decided to take an excursion on a *dhow* and, our swimming gear packed, drove, once again in an irritatingly low gear, over to the harbour where we parked up. Passing rows of orange and yellow fibreglass skiffs floating lifelessly, their outboard motors lifted out of the water, we strolled towards a picturesque dhow moored at the quayside. As we contemplated the hand-written sign propped in front of it advertising trips through the fjords of Musandam with lunch and drinks included, a man, perhaps in his early forties, sprang from the boat and came marching towards us, beaming a salesman's smile, marred slightly by a missing tooth.

'*Salam alaykum!*' he exclaimed, opening his arms. 'How are you?' As he approached us, I noticed a long scar, perhaps from an old knife wound, running along his lower cheek. With a palm on his chest, he introduced himself as Ahmed and in excellent English proceeded to list all the sights we would see were we to take a tour on his vessel.

He was both enthusiastic and persuasive and so we counted out our *rials*, clambered aboard and, after taking our shoes off, made ourselves comfortable on the carpets and the red, black and white striped *majlis* cushions arranged along the gunwales. A couple of scrawny sailors in turbans and folds of white cloth, their skin almost the same colour as the teak of the high-sided *dhow*, walked around the boat, nimbly climbing barefoot along the bulwarks with almost prehensile toes and pulling at ropes with hands older than their years. Ahmed barked a few orders at them before heading towards the stern where a man in a white crocheted *taqiyah* cap was quietly singing. He was busying himself with trays covered in aluminium foil and an assortment of blue plastic bags in which, by craning my neck, I could just see lemons, oranges and Omani flatbread. The dhow was of traditional design and looked as I imagined boats in this part of the world had done for centuries, so I was surprised when a diesel engine suddenly spluttered to life. As we chugged slowly out from the harbour, lying under the shade of the canvas awning that stretched the length of the deck, I looked back towards Khasab as it gradually shrank until it was no more than a strip of cream and white punctuated with green before finally slipping from view.

Once away from the coast, the *dhow* began gently rocking as it ploughed its way east across the jade sea towards the Khor as Sham, one of the impressive fjords which nature has gouged into this remote peninsula that separates the Persian Gulf from the Gulf of Oman. The salty smell of the sea ebbed back and forth on the light breeze that floated over the boat and which occasionally taunted us with the aroma of spices and onions from the makeshift galley at the stern.

'Is this your first time in Oman?' asked Ahmed, coming barefoot across the carpet towards us.

'It is for me,' I answered, glancing towards the helm and relieved to see that one of the other sailors was at the wheel, 'but Frédéric has been here before, in Muscat.'

'Today we will sail to a very nice place,' smiled our captain, sitting down cross-legged in front of us. Only now did I notice his curiously large ears, which, with the light behind them, were almost translucent.

'What about the smugglers?' asked Frédéric, lifting himself into a more upright position, a glint in his eye. During the drive from Dubai he had shown a strange fascination, bordering on the obsessive, with the illicit activities of the Musandam and was clearly keen to find out more.

'We will not see any where we are going!' laughed our host as he picked at one of his toes. 'They only work at night.'

'What do they smuggle?' I asked, trying not to stare at his ears.

'They bring sheep and goats from Iran,' said Ahmed after a long pause. 'It's only forty kilometres from here on the other side of the Strait of Hormuz. They are sent to the UAE. On the way back they take televisions, cigarettes, mobile phones, whatever people bring from Dubai. It's big business here: the town could not survive without it. If you go to the harbour at night you'll find it's very busy, lots of people. Did you see all those little boats?'

'You mean the orange ones?'

'Yes,' Ahmed nodded. 'Those are the boats people use for smuggling. They are very full when they leave Khasab!' He made an arc in the air with his hands as if showing how high the piles of illicit goods were stacked in the skiffs. 'Sometimes people make two or three crossings in a night: they are young so they have a lot of energy and enthusiasm!' he smiled, eyes widening. 'But it's dangerous.'

With his scar and missing tooth, I suddenly felt Ahmed bore an unsettling resemblance to a pirate – or perhaps a smuggler.

'Because of all the ships?' I asked, clearing my throat.

'Yes, you have to be careful of ships, but the big problem is the Iranian coast guard: if they catch you, you're finished.' Ahmed's tone was now more serious and he seemed to be considering his words. 'Or you can pay them money, but that is expensive.' He studied us for a moment with intelligent, probing eyes before getting up. 'Relax and enjoy the view,' he smiled and sauntered back to the helm.

As we approached the fjord, or *khor*, rugged mountains rose on either side, the steep angles of their layers of strata that disappeared into the sea looking like decks on giant, sinking ships. The Arabian Plate, which includes the Musandam Peninsula, is pushing under its Eurasian counterpart, dragging the mountains around the fjord down into the earth. This, together with the sea filling the sinking valleys, is what created the spectacular scenery that surrounded us. The angle may look dramatic, but the speed at which the mountains are sliding beneath the sea is geological: only the occasional earthquake betrays the magnitude of the forces at play. We sailed on, straining our eyes as we looked up at the craggy outcrops and overhangs that cast short shadows on the now turquoise sea. It was strange to be surrounded by water and yet see land that was so dry, so dusty. The parched mountains appeared positively thirsty, ready, like some fabled land worthy of a sailor's yarn, to suck all the moisture out of any soul foolish enough to set foot on them. According to legend, Sinbad once ventured through these waters and it was not hard to imagine the trepidation that these surroundings would have put into the hearts of seafarers of yore and easy to understand why they would fear monsters and fantastic creatures dwelling in such realms. Indeed, as I lay reclined on the cushions in the rising temperature of the late morning, I found myself starting to visualise dancing skeletons appearing on the mountain tops and giant statues in the next bay grinding slowly to life as we sailed into view. Yet how different these mountains would look, I thought, if suddenly rain were to fall often enough to turn dust to moist soil, barren rock becoming green as bushes and flowers sprouted on ledges and slopes, gradually transforming the harsh, inhospitable environment into a gentler, more familiar landscape.

We had left all signs of civilisation behind, once again transported to a barren world that could have been on another planet or in another time. Ahead, the view was hazy in the heat, the mountains no more than smoky shapes lined up one behind the other until they reached the backdrop of the bright grey sky. Somewhere among those peaks was the road to Jebel al Harim along which we had driven the day before. I watched as a short distance away a flock of cormorants, little more than fluttering silhouettes against the fulgent sea, flew past before settling some way ahead, barely making a splash as they landed. We continued to ply the waters of the fjord, the sun finally breaking through the haze as it rose ever higher. By the time we reached Telegraph Island halfway up, a delicious smell of garlic was hanging over the boat as the cook, squatting on his haunches in his camel-coloured *dishdasha*, put the final touches to the buffet lunch. Shading my eyes with my hand, I looked at the uninviting rock where in the nineteenth century British telegraph operators toiled at a repeater station. For years on end, they listened to and retransmitted messages in Morse code sent between London and British India. The story goes that the isolation and boredom of the posting drove the lonely men insane, whither the expression to have 'gone round the bend', the island being just beyond a turn in the empty fjord. Absorbed by the surroundings, I watched the sunlight, dazzling as it danced on the water. Suddenly, the motor stopped and we were surrounded by stillness. One of the sinewy sailors wove his way aft and, with strength surprising for his build, threw the two-fluked anchor overboard, its splash a moment later breaking the silence.

Ahmed told us we could go for a dip before lunch. I peered over the side. It was like looking into an aquarium: dozens of brightly coloured fish were gliding through water so clear I could see the seabed. Minutes later, we were swimming and floating in the deliciously warm fjord with the fearless little fish. Yellow, orange, shimmering silver or with thick iridescent stripes, they greedily nibbled on the chicken drumsticks the captain had given us to feed them. When I was left with little more than a bone to hold, I let it sink and watched the fish dive down after it before I began to swim the short distance to Telegraph Island, while Frédéric clambered back aboard. The rocks near the shore's edge were rough underfoot as I gingerly climbed out of the water. From out at sea, the island had looked to be covered by a thin carpet of grass, but now, close up, I saw that the blades of hardy green were sparsely spread. At the far end, a couple of hundred metres away, stood the crumbling remains of a low building and two or three small trees. I started to head towards them, but the coarse ground proved too painful underfoot. I turned to look at the *dhow* and waved to Frédéric who was watching me, his blond hair reflecting the light. Out of the water and away from the shade, the heat was searing and I could feel my skin beginning to burn. I picked my way back over the sharp rocks and, like an ungainly merman desperate to return to more comfortable surroundings, slipped into the welcoming sea.

Back on board, I dried myself off and joined Frédéric and Ahmed at the stern where the cook had set out lunch. We stuffed ourselves with chicken, saffron-scented rice and salad and tore off pieces of flatbread to scoop up the fresh hummus, its delicious mix of lemon and garlic flavours making self-restraint impossible. I ate far more than I should have, and quickly began to feel sleepy. The cook handed round a plate with oranges, but I could not eat any more. As we weighed anchor and set off back to Khasab we again made ourselves comfortable on the firm cushions and watched as we once more passed the mountains and a small settlement I had not noticed on the way out, perhaps because I had been on the other side of the boat. It was made up of little more than a dozen or so cream-coloured buildings interspersed with palm trees and telegraph poles. There being no obvious road to the coastal village, I reckoned the few boats moored along the shore were probably the only means for its inhabitants to reach the outside world. In my state of digestive torpor, I found myself momentarily musing how bucolic life must be in such a remote place, far away from the pressure and strains of modern-day living. But, as we sailed on, I realised that one man's holiday idyll was another's prison and what, for me, might be an escape from stress could for those living there be absence of opportunity. My mind wandered to Ali and Sayyid and I wondered where they would be in twenty years' time.

Just as I was drifting into daydreams, there was an excited cry from Ahmed. In an instant, one of the sailors was kneeling down beside us, pointing a weathered hand enthusiastically out to sea and repeating something in Arabic. Suddenly alert, I strained my eyes and saw dark forms curving out of the water and then slipping back beneath the waves: it was a pod of dolphins. We watched as they swam first together, then apart, before they disappeared for a while. Searching the shimmering sea until our eyes ached, we eventually saw them resurface further away. It was almost as good as seeing a leopard and I could feel the warmth of a smile spreading over my face. As they dived for the last time before vanishing from view, I had the sensation of having witnessed a minor miracle, these beautiful creatures managing to survive so near to one of the world's busiest waterways. It reminded me of their cousins I had seen some years earlier in the Bosphorus, another shipping thoroughfare and an equally surprising spot to see these graceful animals.

As we sailed back into Khasab, we thanked Ahmed and the crew, who waved us goodbye as warmly as if we were life-long friends. It felt like we had been away for days not just hours, and on a journey to another world, not merely round the bend. The sun was now an orange orb descending slowly into the sea. On my skin I could feel where it had cast its gaze and the waters of the Persian Gulf had left their salty dust: it had been a wonderful day at sea, but different from others.

In the evening, showered and changed, we ventured out into Khasab. The main settlement of Oman's tiniest governorate is not much more than a little town, its 18,000 residents inhabiting an uninspiring collection of buildings spread out on the flat valley floor. Asphalted roads carved up the sandy ground into triangles, squares and other geometrical shapes, each containing a few buildings or a walled garden with trees. Otherwise, the part of town between the harbour and the toy-sized airport was surprisingly verdant, groves of thick-trunked date palms providing a real sense of oasis beneath the arid mountains. The commercial centre, known as the new souk, was made up of three or four rows of shabby stores in whitewashed buildings, together with a post office and a barber shop. The parades were separated by an open space where, in the fading light, we parked alongside a collection of dusty vehicles. A few drooping trees and thorn bushes that had escaped foraging by goats helped brighten up what was a rather depressing sight. We wandered along the parade of brightly lit shops in which wholesale packs of food and bottles of soft drinks were piled high under polythene wrap and where ultraviolet bug zappers fizzed and buzzed on tired walls. Other stores, with signs outside euphemistically describing them as 'trading' or 'import-export' companies, were empty except for a battered desk, a couple of chairs and swarthy men hanging around and talking. They looked at us blankly, their moustaches ceasing to twitch as they stopped conversations to watch us amble by.

Finding little of interest, we went back to our 4x4 and drove the short distance inland to the old souk. Predictably for such a small town, it turned out to be modest in size. We strolled around looking at boxes of spices, beads, scarves and clay incense burners from behind which the stallholders studied us intently. At one of the stands, I picked up a *jerz*, a type of axe unique to Musandam that I had read about, and wondered whether it would make an interesting souvenir or just add to the clutter at home. The old man to whose modest collection of wares it belonged sat in silence as I examined the steel axe-head engraved with traditional diamond and chevron designs. He watched me, dark, mouse-like eyes peering out from a leathery face as I ran my fingers across the metal, trying to overcome my ambivalence about anything with a dangerous blade. The almond wood handle into which lines and crosses had been carefully carved was smooth to the touch and as long as my arm. A *jerz* was once an essential tool for chopping firewood, using as a walking stick on the rugged terrain, or for fending off caracal lynx or leopards, when there was still a reasonable chance of seeing one. Today, the distinctive hatchet is still a key accessory for men here, but, I decided, one I could do without. Smiling at the stallholder, I returned the axe to the top of the rough tea chest where I had found it. He played with his matted beard and nodded almost imperceptibly, his eyes now avoiding direct contact with my own.

The next day, we visited the old fort built by the Portuguese, a square construction near the sea with a squat tower at each corner of its thick, rendered walls and a red, white and green Omani flag hanging languidly from a pole. We walked past a couple of old *dhows* propped on stands and made our way along the crazy paving path which formed a sort of neatly bordered causeway over a sea of grey gravel. On either side of the ogee-arched entrance stood an old canon and over the dark brown double doors was a sign marked 'Khasab Castle', above which a line of Arab calligraphy curved like a scimitar. The iconic fort had been meticulously restored and offered an image of perfection far removed from what life could ever have been like in the seventeenth century. The brochure said it was originally a supply station for Portuguese ships that would stop off to stock up on water and dates as they navigated their way through the straits. Now, in the tidy courtyard with its crazy paving, small fishing boats were balanced on stands, oars resting against their sides, notices in front of them detailing their features. We made our way round the circular tower in the centre, which proudly predates both the stronghold and the Lusitanians, and headed towards a couple of palm trees where we took advantage of the shade. Diagonally across from us, four slender men in smart white *dishdashas*, red-chequered *kefiyehs* and large sunglasses, were looking in an open doorway. They strolled round the courtyard, mobile phones in their hands, chatting and pausing occasionally to read the various signs that explained the fort's history or described exhibits.

We slowly ascended the steps to the crenellated battlements where we wandered along looking at the dense groves of date palms that extended inland through the town. I could feel the top of my head burning and wished I had brought a hat. From the loudspeakers of a blue-domed mosque a short distance away, the *adhan* began, the voice of the muezzin echoing out over the rooftops and the plantations until it seemed to reach the surrounding mountains themselves. The majority of Omanis are Ibadi, a conservative form of Islam separate from Sunnis and Shias and another layer in the special identity felt by the people here. I find the call to prayer atmospheric, but it has never held the same appeal for me as it does for Frédéric. Anyone watching him listen to the lyrical voice could have been forgiven for thinking he understood every word. We continued along the parapet until we were facing the fishing wharf with its rows of little blue and white boats and, further on, the main harbour from where we had sailed the day before. Beyond, stretched the green waters of the Strait of Hormuz and, somewhere in the haze, the shores of Iran. Standing in this sleepy corner of Oman, it was strange to think we were so near to the shipping lanes through which a third of the world's oil passes. The *adhan* finished, the echo of the muezzin's last words faded quickly and silence once again descended on the little town of Khasab.

It was time to head back to Dubai, but first we wanted to pick up some water for the journey. The engine growled deeply as we trundled along the almost deserted streets towards the uninspiring rows of shops we had visited the previous evening. I looked at the houses as we passed by, mostly simple constructions little more than concrete boxes, some painted white or cream, a few decorated with a satellite dish or a wrought-iron flourish around the windows. Two figures walking towards us on the other side of the road caught my eye: small boys hand in hand, one a head taller than the other. As we got nearer, I recognised them as Ali and Sayyid, their school bags on their backs. They did not see us behind the tinted glass and a moment later we had driven by, a large white vehicle like any other. I wondered if someone had given them a lift into town at the start of the new school week or whether, when they sat down at their desks, they would already be exhausted from the long trek, their dusty feet aching. I was impressed by their, or their parents', determination that they get an education, but was saddened at the thought of the few possibilities I imagined were available to them. The field of opportunities was, I supposed, probably as barren as the mountains that surrounded the town, the chances of major change as likely as regular rainfall coming to this corner of Arabia. Some years hence, might Ali and Sayyid be the ones taking tourists out to the *khor*, I wondered, proudly showing them the stark beauty of their region, or would they, like so many others, end up risking imprisonment, or even their lives, as smugglers? I would never know whether they would grow up seeing their tiny Omani enclave as a scenic oasis in which they felt fortunate to live, or as a harsh, rocky prison devoid of prospects. Yet, I realised, my imaginings of what the two boys might want or aspire to were no more than personal dreams, a product of my own worldview. And I could no more change their lives than I could the climate. With a fanfare of revs we pulled up in front of one of the tiny stores in the town centre, Frédéric delighting in the noise of the engine. A short while later, provisions acquired, we bade farewell to Khasab and set off on our way back to Dubai, the Land Cruiser purring on the newly-asphalted road as I slipped into top gear.

119

Marguerites of Hope

'I take it as a sign from God,' declares the vicar at the far end of the church, 'that there is hope for this city and for this country, that on today, Good Friday, He should send us tourists.'

Speaking into a microphone, the interpreter translates his words into Arabic as the small congregation gathered in the first rows listens intently. In front of me, a young soldier, barely out of his teens, wearing grey camouflage fatigues and a black SWAT vest, stands watching and listening, an AK47 held loosely in front of him, a black beret tucked in his pocket. His thick, wavy hair is not shaved in the military fashion you might expect, making him look as if he has been hurriedly dressed up in a uniform rather than trained in a boot camp.

'Of course, they must be mad,' the vicar adds light-heartedly, 'but we are all mad here, aren't we!'

When they hear the translation, a ripple of laughter goes through the crowd: they are used to his jokes. If anyone needs a sense of humour in addition to their faith, it is these people: over the years, nearly three hundred of the congregation have been slaughtered by bombs and bullets, but in the face of such threats you have a choice of keeping your spirits up or sinking into the black hole of depression. The service is informal: children wander up and down the slightly dusty plum-coloured carpet that stretches the length of the aisle, while a flat-screen TV on a stand next to the chancel shows changing images of Christ, now on the cross, now preaching, now on the cross again.

As the plane began its descent I was struck by how flat everywhere was and how green, canals and waterways stretching into the distance and disappearing into the early morning haze. I had imagined a country of endless dust and sand as shown unremittingly on television, but, as I was to discover, there were many aspects of life on the ground that were different to the images that the media choose to show us. Looking at the verdant fields and the palm groves below, I felt the heartbeat of excitement: after some hesitation, not to say trepidation, I was here at last. I was about to arrive in the land of Adam, Abraham and Alexander the Great, in the land where the world's first cities rose from fertile plains, where it all started, where the wheel and writing were invented, where the first piece of literature in human history was written, a country whose past cultures left a legacy that forms the basis of much of our world today: I was about to arrive in Iraq.

A beautiful, haunting song unlike any I have heard reverberates around the church, its exotic tones contrasting with the building's sober interior of sand-coloured bricks and its simple, white arched ceiling. Voices sing in a language I do not recognise; the music sounds as if transported from antiquity. The service seems to have more of a rolling, ongoing nature rather than being limited to a specific event. Taking a break from the ceremony, the vicar comes down the aisle, passing the mostly empty wooden pews, accompanied by several children. They are smiling and relaxed as if unaware of the turbulent world outside the confines of the church's compound. The vicar stops in front of us, a tall forty-something figure with lively brown eyes and short swept back hair. A large steel cross hangs on a chain round his neck. Made of two square-headed nails fused together, it looks more like some piece of modern Scandinavian jewellery than a religious icon. A small boy in blue shorts and an orange polo top, his skin darker than the others, leans against the vicar, who puts an arm gently round his shoulder. The children gravitate to Andrew White with genuine affection.

'Welcome to St. George's,' he says. 'It's lovely to have you here.'

A visit to Baghdad is not like a trip to other capitals in the Middle East: this is not a place to wander around freely, to explore the sights or souks at your leisure; it is not even a place for which, under normal circumstances, you will get a tourist visa. Bombs, shootings, soldiers, angry mobs, wailing women and blood-spattered streets: that is probably what you associate with Baghdad. Yes, this is what the city is about, but only in part and, with notable exceptions, many of these images increasingly belong to the past. Slowly, in a rather un-newsworthy fashion, despite sporadic and tragic bombings, the security situation is improving. Yet it is indicative of the power of the media that for many of us these are the visions of Iraq that remain seared into our memories. Perhaps, like many of my friends, you imagine a country in ruins with shelled buildings and craters in the roads. When I returned home they asked me if the destruction was very widespread. What bomb damage I did see was mostly from terrorist attacks, not allied bombing. Let me tell you, for the most part, Iraq was simply dilapidated, its ugly, late-twentieth-century concrete buildings gradually falling into disrepair. Almost three decades of wars and sanctions have taken their toll on the economy: for a country rich in black gold, the overwhelming impression was one of poverty and of people struggling to eke out a living for themselves and a better future for their children. Yet signs of improvement were there if you looked for them. As we drove down one of the many new motorway slip roads, I saw workmen toiling away in the loop it made to create an area with park benches and flower beds. Perhaps to you or me the idea of spending an afternoon next to a flyover might seem odd, but public spaces and parks are few and far between in this city of seven million inhabitants, second in the Arab world only to Cairo. The large-scale reconstruction of the country is accompanied by a determined attempt to return to normality. That is what most people here want.

'It's quite an eventful day with it being Good Friday,' says Canon White, 'although it's a bit quieter just at the moment, so I was able to step out. It'll get busy again later. Come in and have a chat.' His powerful voice has a strange lilt to it, making his speech sound slightly slurred.

Accompanied by Omar, the ever-smiling guide and interpreter from the Ministry of Tourism, as well as Captain Hassan and Sergeant Ahmed, two plain-clothes guards sent by the Ministry of the Interior, we head along the paved pathway that transects the dry grass towards the gate leading to the vicarage garden. Here, the well-tended lawn is a brighter, more nourished green, flanked by a few thin rosebushes planted at intervals along the green metal fence. A handful of roses – pink, yellow and red – peep out from among the thorns and dark green leaves. It would be a normal, if somewhat sparse, garden for a vicarage if it were not for what stands in the centre. I pause to look at the white marble cenotaph, a trapezoid rising solemnly from a circle of stones and more rosebushes. On it, below an inscription from the Bible, are the names of Danish soldiers killed on duty here. I look at the list: three of them were only twenty when they died. Towering behind it, beyond the wall surrounding the compound, is the rusting skeleton of a bombed-out office building with half its walls missing and, above it, a peaceful blue sky with picture-book wisps of white cloud.

We turn the corner of the vicarage, a rectangular, single-storey building of beige and whitewashed bricks whose only concession to architectural style consists of two arches at the corner porch. We enter by a side door into what looks like a doctor's waiting room. A large, overwhelmingly dark portrait of a bearded Abraham, the prophet revered by Christians, Muslims and Jews alike, hangs on one of the walls, a fitting decoration: the man lived in the city of Ur, the crumbling mud brick ruins of which lie in southern Iraq. Clutching the zip-up faux leather file with our papers that never seems to leave his hand, Omar looks round at the spartan room. The canon's teenage helpers start rearranging the plastic chairs so that we are facing him when he sits down on one of the two sofas. It is only now that I notice he is using a walking stick.

'Would you like something to drink?' he asks.

The traffic was at a virtual standstill. Omar explained there had been a dramatic rise in car ownership since the end of the war. That and ubiquitous police road blocks, including at the end of every bridge over the Tigris, made getting around the city a slow and unpredictable task. We arrived at a roundabout where myriad yellow taxis of an unknown make were managing to weave their way through the traffic, dodging the occasional shiny 4x4 or sweating barrow boy pushing a crippling load. I laughed as we passed a fibreglass shelter for traffic police with a roof in the shape of a vastly oversized policeman's peaked cap below which a black tie descended and projected at the bottom to form a seat where the officer on duty could sit observing the traffic. Somebody in the Ministry of

Transport, it seemed, had a sense of humour. It was strange to think that somewhere in the world – perhaps in Iraq – there was a factory churning out these comical shelters.

We turned into a boulevard lined with rundown apartment blocks, six-storey monstrosities in depressing brown, their windows small, their walls lined with ageing air-conditioner box units. The architecture was distinctly 1970s and 1980s when much of the city was rebuilt, seemingly in the style of some of Europe's worst experiments with social housing. Small trees, misshapen with age, coloured fairy lights adorning their branches, lined the road. Everywhere among the lingering brutality, be it that of the security situation or that of the urban planners, were signs of a craving for normality, for happier times.

Eventually, we reached a bridge and stopped at the police check point, a hut with a red and white rising arm barrier surrounded by concrete traffic dividers. Rather incongruously, like the roadside trees, the barrier had fairy lights wrapped round it and on the dividers someone had painted what looked like yellow and white marguerites, the flowers that adorned Babylon's Ishtar Gate, the flowers that symbolise innocence. A garland of lurid green imitation leaves draped along the top provided a finishing touch. I reached for my camera.

'No photographs here, please.' Underlying Omar's friendly voice was a timbre of nervousness.

There was something touching about the scene, an almost childlike optimism and a yearning for the simple pleasures in life instead of the adrenalin and stress that comes from policing a city stalked by sectarian violence. Omar had told me that Iraqis, men and women alike, loved flowers: in front of me was an example at once sad and uplifting. As I watched the policemen in their camouflage fatigues chatting to our driver Mazen while they inspected our papers, I tried to imagine them carefully painting marguerites on to the drab concrete. Mazen, a tall man with a large nose and a cheeky smile, casually rested his hairy arm on the open window as he answered their questions. Leaning across, Hassan said something to the police sergeant holding the papers and a moment later we were waved on our way. With the traffic on the bridge so regulated, there were few vehicles as we drove across the fast-flowing Tigris. The turbid river was an unappealing brown, but its breadth meant we had a good view up- and downstream of what is still very much a low-rise city.

'That is the Green Zone,' said Omar, pointing a chubby finger back towards the right bank, but from where we were I could not make out any features that distinguished the fortified sector from the surrounding area.

One of the canon's young helpers returns from the adjoining kitchen with a tray of cold cans of Coke, Fanta and Sprite. It is not quite afternoon tea at the vicarage, but this is not quite St Mary Mead either. The girl, a slight figure, is dressed as anyone her age in Europe would be. Smiling, she holds the tray in front of us as we each take one of the slim 25cl cans and a straw. The ring-pulls are the old-fashioned variety that come off rather than fold back; once again, I silently curse a Western manufacturer for using lower standards in a developing country.

'So I suppose you would like to know a bit about St George's,' says the canon, adjusting his rectangular glasses and politely turning down a fizzy drink as the girl passes in front of him. She puts the tray down on the glass coffee table and joins the half-dozen other young people who have gathered in the room and now stand against one of its white-plastered walls, listening intently.

'It's the only Anglican church in Baghdad, but, in fact, only Faiz the curate and I are actually Anglican: nearly everybody else is Syriac Orthodox, but we have a few Catholics and other denominations who come along too. Everyone is welcome.'

I glance at Hassan and Ahmed. They are sitting politely, ankles crossed, hands in their laps, pretending to listen, but their English is less than rudimentary: our communication is through a mixture of single words and sign language or through Omar. Ahmed, at twenty-eight the younger but more corpulent of the two, has already finished his Coke and leans across to put the empty can on the coffee table.

'The church itself was first constructed in 1864,' continues the canon, 'but, as you've probably noticed from the sign at the entrance, the current building dates from 1936. It was badly damaged when the two car bombs went off in 2009, but everyone has worked very hard to repair it.'

'How big is the congregation?' I ask.

'About 4,000,' he replies. 'Sadly, 273 of them have been killed in the last five years. We miss them all; it's very difficult for the Christians here, for everyone, but our faith keeps us going.' Even when speaking of tragedy he somehow exudes a positive aura and I begin to understand why the people here seem drawn to him. 'But it's not just the Christians,' he continues, 'it's the Sunnis, the Shias, the Mandaeans: everyone is targeted.'

'Why?'

'Because they are different from those who are targeting them. Of course, the main conflict is between the Sunnis and Shias, but everyone else is caught up in it. My entire church council was killed and my head of security had his legs blown off. As you can see, though, the Iraqi government provides me with a lot of security.'

I look at the young soldier standing casually in the open doorway and pause to reflect: like Andrew White, he and his colleagues are risking their lives every day.

'How long have you been working here?' As the words leave my mouth I hear how superficial and facile my question sounds compared to the gravity of his last statement.

'Fourteen years. I divide my time between St George's and Guildford where my wife and two sons live. This is a very special place, though: the people are wonderful. And I've five adopted children here.' His eyes twinkle, lips widening into a generous smile on his round face.

The key to terrorism, of course, is fear: fear of the unknown, of wondering whether today will be the day when the dice of fate will roll and you will join so many others as a gruesome statistic. I was not frightened as we walked through the street market in Baghdad, but I was aware that the odds were slightly more weighted than usual. Yet I was only there for a visit, while those around me, the storeholders and shoppers, the children and police, had to run the gauntlet of sectarian violence on a daily basis. These people came here regularly in the knowledge that one day a bomb, perhaps in a parked vehicle, maybe strapped to a suicide bomber and filled with nails, might explode and yet they managed to keep their spirits up and chat and laugh. Perhaps having bodyguards lulled me into a false sense of security: they could offer protection against an aggressive individual, but if a bomb went off they would be as likely to fall victim as I was. To my eye, with their casual shirts over their jeans and their pointed shoes, Hassan and Ahmed at first looked like many other Iraqi men: you could not even see the Austrian-made *Glock* handguns they had tucked in their jeans, one on either side and each loaded with fifteen rounds. After a while, though, I began to notice that their demeanour was subtly different from that of the middle-aged Omar, whose carefree amble was in contrast to the considered manner of the two guards who discreetly observed everything around us. Both were jovial enough, though Captain Hassan was a little more reserved, but I gradually realised that they would have no qualms about using their guns if necessary: in Baghdad, hesitation is not an option.

At first, the food market appeared to be pure chaos: stands at each side of the street seemed in competition with people selling wares from the open backs of vans, empty cardboard boxes formed jumbled mountains and old men and young boys struggled to manoeuvre overloaded handcarts past shuffling pedestrians and across rickety boards spanning open drains. There was plenty of food, but little choice. The range was limited to potatoes, beans, onions, bananas, oranges, apples and watermelons, yet much of the fruit was arranged in meticulously neat piles. The sellers were as proud as their wooden stands were modest. I stopped to look at a row of open bowls of olives – black, purple and green, some as big as walnuts – and boxes of dried apricots, plums and figs. Both displays seemed to attract more flies than customers. The stallholder looked at me with curiosity; his lean form and deeply tanned skin spoke of a much harder life than I could ever imagine. I contemplated how the alter ego of this quiet man might also have been one of the myriad faces in the rioting crowds so beloved of television cameras. Extending a sinewy hand towards a bowl of large green olives, he smiled encouragingly. It was a kind gesture, which I turned down as gracefully as I could by returning the smile, shaking my head and using one of the few words of Arabic I know: *shukran*, thank you. We moved on and a little further passed a couple of small butchers' shops where just two or three cuts of meat hung in the open window; one large piece had some entrails dangling from it, perhaps the heart. My thoughts drifted to the conditions under which I imagined livestock were slaughtered in this country.

Suddenly, taking my arm, Hassan, the shorter of the two guards, pulled me aside as a large camouflage army vehicle, some sort of armoured personnel carrier, rumbled past, each of the four wheels on either side almost as high as my waist.

'Careful!' he said, looking up at me with a smile.

Sitting atop at the back were two soldiers, silently observing the people around them through their mirror sunglasses, automatic weapons by their side. None of the locals returned the interest: for the shoppers of Baghdad, such sights have become wallpaper.

'There are only seven Jews left in Iraq,' explains Canon White, 'not counting those in the US embassy. There are more there than in the rest of the country.'

I reflect on this state of affairs. I know Judaism has a long and mixed history in Mesopotamia, including the captivity in Babylon under Nebuchadnezzar twenty-six centuries ago, a seminal moment in Jewish lore. It is tragic that there is no space for Jews here today and, indeed, ever less for Christians.

'I have a doctorate in Judaism. Yes, rather odd for an Anglican priest, isn't it!' the canon laughs, as he sees the surprise on our faces. 'I actually conduct the Jewish services in the American embassy, you know. I'm doing Passover for them too. Everyone thinks of Iraq as a Muslim country which, of course, for the most part today it is, but so much of the Bible, especially the Old Testament, took place here, you know.' He looks at us. 'Have you been to the Garden of Eden yet?'

'No,' says Omar, 'but we will.'

'You should! Of course, it has lost some of its original charm,' the canon remarks dryly, 'but it's still worth going. There is so much to see here: Babylon is fascinating, even though it did not get a particularly good write-up in the Bible. You can see the spot there where Alexander the Great died. The country is full of churches, you know. Saint Thomas lived in Mosul before moving on to India, although it's best avoided at the moment, but I'm sure you know that. It's such a tragedy because until fairly recently there was much more tolerance here towards Jews, Christians, Mandaeans and all the other groups. Many have simply emigrated even though their communities have been here for centuries.'

I notice that when he is not smiling his lips turn down slightly at the corners. I am not surprised. However strong one's faith, however much of a brave face one puts on it, living and working here must surely bring stress as well as satisfaction.

We left the food market and made our way along a narrow lane lined with shops selling garish nylon cocktail dresses, drab T-shirts for men and hideous tops and leggings for women with motifs that looked as if they had been copied from 1960s wallpaper. Business seemed slow: the shop workers, all male, stood in the doorways looking bored or sat at desks, playing on their mobile phones or reading newspapers. The street was fairly busy, but nobody seemed to be stopping to look at the goods on show, even less buying them. A youth called out in Arabic, clearly wanting everyone to move aside, as he pushed his way past, carefully balancing a large aluminium tray of buns on his head. He walked briskly and purposefully through the narrow street, continuing to announce his presence to the shoppers as he went on his way. Among the people milling about a young girl in a black *abaya* caught my eye. She must have been only six or seven years old and yet was covered by the shapeless garment adult women wear to prevent men from supposedly being driven wild with lust by the sight of female contours. I asked myself why a prepubescent child should have to dress in such clothes, but none of the answers that came to mind was pleasant.

Omar stopped to ask one of the older shopkeepers if he knew where the synagogue was. The man raised his thick eyebrows and rubbed his chin whilst looking at us as if wondering whether to cooperate or not. Then, with the aid of gestures, he began explaining the route. Omar beckoned us to follow and we continued a little further along dog-leg bends before turning into a sort of dim corridor linking one street to another. Empty boxes lay around and cables ran the length of the grubby walls, the light seeping in from either end just enough for us to pick our way through the shadows. We emerged into a lane, which was so narrow that from the bay windows of the houses you could easily lean out and shake hands with someone in the window opposite. Sadly, the traditional Iraqi homes that lined the short section are an increasingly rare sight in Baghdad. The street soon widened out and we found ourselves standing between a small, nondescript apartment building and the open entrance to a walled yard full of noisy machinery.

'I think this is it,' said Omar, waving a tanned arm in the direction of the workshop.

We wandered into the yard. Two rows of diesel-powered machines, apparently generators of some sort and each as high as a man, roared away on either side. It felt like walking into a furnace. Buckets, oily rags, and bits of equipment lay everywhere. A man, sweating in a dirty vest, appeared in a doorway at the far end, his mouth forming inaudible words. Omar went up to him and, trying to make himself heard over the din of the machines, explained we were looking for the old synagogue. The man nodded, looked around and then pointed to somewhere beyond the engines. Omar strolled back to where we stood, his face now glowing with perspiration.

'This is the old synagogue,' he said, almost shouting to make himself heard. 'The man says we can look around. Over there in the corner he says you can see some Jewish writing and signs.'

I looked up at the crumbling walls that rose on either side of the yard and tried to imagine what the building might have looked like when it was a functioning place of worship. Beige plaster crumbled away to reveal rough brickwork, and a network of wires and cables criss-crossed the sky. We followed Omar to the far end of the yard and then passed between the sweating, roaring machines. Beyond the generators was a doorway leading to what looked like a storeroom where, in the gloom, I could see a stack of plastic crates. On one side of the door was the rough plaster outline of a Star of David, on the other I could just make out some Hebrew writing. This was all that remained of the last synagogue in Baghdad.

'We have a wonderful clinic here,' says the canon. 'We even have a dentist. Like the church, the clinic was badly damaged in the 2009 bombing, but we have managed to repair and restore it and now we treat about 2,000 people a month. It is also one of the best clinics in the world for stem cell work.'

Again, I find myself trying not to look surprised.

'Yes, you wouldn't think so, would you?' he grins. 'We have people come from all over the world to get treatment here: more than 3,700 so far. Of course, we don't do transplants; it's all done with the patient's own stem cells. I was the first to be treated, in fact. A friend said I should try it for my multiple sclerosis and it has worked wonders. They can't really do anything for my deafness, though,' he smiles.

Now I understand the walking stick and the slight slurring of speech. Suddenly, I am aware of being in the presence of a truly remarkable man.

We turned down another street lined with concrete blast walls and 1980s government buildings, some seemingly in use, others obviously empty. Trees, planted in another era when Baghdad was a city of leafy boulevards, provided greenery and a soft contrast to the prison-like concrete of the neighbourhood. We drove slowly, stopping at one check point after another, each time the heavily armed policemen checking the papers our driver showed them. Eventually, in a narrow side street, we stopped next to a grey prefab hut shaded by a couple of large trees. A dozen or so soldiers were milling around, while another, smoking a cigarette, was sitting on one of the battered plastic chairs that were lined up in front of the makeshift guardhouse. Most of them were wearing black SWAT jackets over their grey camouflage fatigues. Heavy calibre weaponry abounded.

We got out and Omar, Hassan and Ahmed greeted their countrymen, shaking hands with the officers. Papers were shown and we were nodded through, accompanied by one of the soldiers. Wearing a black beret, he was little more than a boy and eyed us with curiosity. Entering the garden of the modest compound with its trimmed bushes, we headed up the path that ran alongside the hedge towards the far end of the building. Among the bedding plants were some rather straggly marguerites, their fragile flowers adding a touch of colour among the greenery. Moments later, we arrived at the main entrance where steps led up to the two wooden doors to the side of which was a plaque. I moved forward to get a better view. The red outline of a knight on a horse spearing a dragon was accompanied by text in Arabic and in English: 'St George's Episcopal Anglican Church, Built 1936'. As we headed up the steps of the beige brick building, the vicar, dressed in a perfectly ironed black cassock, appeared.

'Hello!' he said, as warmly as if we were regular parishioners. 'Now, I must say, you don't look as if you live here.'

'No,' I replied, 'we're tourists.'

He laughed loudly.

'Well, you'd better come in then. I'm just about to conduct the service. Do join us.'

A Strange Immortality

Tell me, have you ever visited somewhere famous or steeped in history and afterwards found that your abiding memory of the place is not of a monument or spectacular building, but of something else, something seemingly insignificant or small, something human? This happened to me in Aleppo. Let me tell you about it.

Like many cities in the Middle East, Aleppo has been continuously inhabited for millennia, perhaps since 5000 BC, a mind-numbing period if you try to calculate the number of generations who were born and have lived and died here: maybe as many as four hundred. Unsurprisingly, Halab, to give it its Arab name, is a *millefeuille* of human settlement in the region made up of layer upon layer of history. The catalogue of powers that have ruled or governed the city reads like the contents list of an encyclopaedia of great civilisations and empires: Greeks and Romans, Sassanids and Mongols, Byzantines and Turcomen, Ottomans and French, and many others besides. Alexander the Great, Saladin and Tamerlane each succeeded in wresting control of the city, yet, if they are remembered today, it is not for their conquest of Aleppo. The crusaders, on the other hand, twice tried and failed to take the city, and the names of few of them, if any, have survived the passage of time. Yet, many of those who came to Aleppo did leave their mark here: in its architecture, in its art, in its music, and in its food. Some, as I was to discover, left an enduring legacy of a different sort.

I arrived after driving from Hama, a small town some 150 kilometres to the south renowned for two things: its giant wooden water wheels, or *norias*, that churn slowly in the Orontes River with a distinctive cracking, creaking sound and, rather less picturesquely, the 1982 Hama Massacre when government troops shot thousands of the city's inhabitants. Aleppo was the latest stop on a tour of Syria I made when the Assad regime's position was still unchallenged. Top of my 'must see' list were the city's vast medieval citadel and its celebrated souk, of which I had heard so many stories. I had a map and a mobile phone, but locating my hotel was a challenge and I found myself going back and forth along the same stretch of road outside the old centre desperately trying to join up the hotel receptionist's directions with the nondescript concrete buildings around me. Finally, I came across a patch of rough land full of parked cars at the far end of which stood *Bab al-Qinnesrin*, one of the nine city gates hewn from the nougat-coloured limestone out of which much of old Aleppo is built. I parked up and headed into the heart of the historic city, wheeling my duffel bag behind me as the gentle November sun slipped towards the horizon. The dimensions of the imposing gate were deceptive: the actual entrance was only accessible on foot or with a handcart. I made my way through the shadowy vaulted chambers of the gateway. In one, a handful of youths lingered in the darker recesses, their whispers ceasing as I walked past; the only noise was of pigeons fluttering up to barely visible ledges. I emerged blinking into the former Christian quarter of the Old City, my luggage bumping and bouncing along the uneven paving stones of the narrow street. An old man in a traditional long, grey *thobe* and a white crocheted *taqiyah* on his head looked at me with bemusement as he walked past, half a dozen neatly folded *dishdashas* under his arm, whilst a group of young boys in blue school uniform smiled a cheerful 'Hello!'

The entrance to the hotel was unpromising, not to say alarming: a narrow stone corridor that sloped downwards into darkness, it looked more like the opening to a pharaoh's tomb. I took a deep breath and stepped into it, a sensor-triggered light immediately revealing an old wooden portal at the end. I rang the bell and moments later the door creaked open, a slim man in his forties beckoning me inside with a hand so hairy it looked like a tarantula crawling out from the end of his suit sleeve. In perfect English he introduced himself as Nazim and bade me enter. As is often the case in the Middle East, the building's unassuming exterior gave nothing away as to the wonders concealed behind its simple walls. After just a few paces following Nazim's silhouette, I found myself in the courtyard of a beautifully restored sixteenth-century merchant's palace. In this dusty corner of Syria, it was a hidden oasis of chic where a bubbling fountain and an *iwan* – the three-sided portal open at the front and typical of Islamic architecture – invited me to forget the world outside and come and relax on the rows of satin cushions along its walls. The courageous investment its owners had made was testimony to their belief in Aleppo's potential as a tourist destination. Nazim smiled when he saw my face, his cold green eyes glowing with satisfaction.

That night, in a nearby restaurant, I reflected on a grand city's gradual decline into relative obscurity. I asked myself how some of today's metropolises would be seen a few centuries hence and wondered if they, too, would be relegated to being historical 'also rans' as power waxed and waned and trade routes changed. As I scooped up a mouthful of garlicky hummus with a piece of hot flatbread, a waiter asked me if I was enjoying my meal. Looking up to reply, I was surprised to see not a swarthy Arab but a fair-skinned man with red hair. And he was not the last I was to see in Aleppo.

The next day, I set off to explore Syria's largest city. Busy and bustling, and with a population a third bigger than the capital Damascus, Aleppo still feels overwhelmingly provincial. The opening of the Suez Canal in 1869 saw trade that had previously passed through the city being carried by ship instead. During the

1920s Turkish War of Independence, Ataturk seized a large chunk of territory from the newly established state of Syria, meaning much of the city's natural hinterland lies on the wrong side of the border. The result is that it is no longer the commercial and cultural crossroads it used to be. To the visitor, the sense of isolation is heightened by the fact that Aleppo sits in a far corner of a country off the main tourist circuit.

My first stop was the famous citadel, the *Qal'at Halab*, a massive limestone construction based around an elliptical hill and surrounded by the remains of a vast twelfth-century moat, dangerously deep, unwelcomingly wide. Human settlement of the hill dates back to the third millennium BC, but it was not until some two thousand years later that the first fortress was built. The size of the fortifications that, even today, dominate Aleppo leave you in no doubt as to the one-time importance of the citadel and the city at the centre of which it stands. Most of the impressive remains that now rose in front of me dated from the Ayyubid dynasty founded in the twelfth century by that most famous of the crusaders' foes, Saladin. As I wandered up the long stone bridge, its six high and slender arches leading from the outer to the inner gate, I found myself imagining bloodthirsty battles of yore with swarms of foot soldiers storming the castle under a hail of whishing arrows. Inside the main gateway, the passage took one right angle turn after another, a ploy exercised to make life difficult for invaders, not least by preventing the use of battering rams. Above me, machicolations served as a grim reminder of the boiling liquids that those inside used to pour onto attackers trying to seize the castle. I paused and contemplated the violence that would once have filled the tranquil space in which I now stood: the shouts and cries of man and beast, the sound of metal upon metal as swords clashed again and again, the stomping of countless marching feet – quite simply, the sounds of siege.

Now, as I stood there, the battles and bloodshed were no more and if the ghosts of those who died fighting here wandered the ruins they did so without leaving the faintest trace of sorrow or melancholy. The citadel, partly restored at the beginning of this century, was a peaceful place and grass and wild flowers grew where the inhabitants of this city-within-a-city once went about their daily business. Young couples sat quietly on the low stone walls, discreetly holding hands and casting furtive glances as I walked past. I made my way slowly round the rocks and rubble, pausing now and again to gaze at the urban sprawl below, the noise of its traffic seeming to belong to a different world. Nowadays, Aleppo, home to over two million people, extends across an area unimaginable to the ancestors of its current citizens. Looking out from the ramparts, I tried to imagine how somebody from centuries ago would react upon seeing the vast city as it is today. Beyond the historic core, Aleppo is not a pretty sight: seen from the hilltop fortress, it is but one more beige metropolis, something in which the Middle East excels.

Just beyond the citadel lies the souk, a veritable Aladdin's cave in which it is difficult not to get lost. Numerous friends, assuring me it was a highlight not to be missed, had raved about its authenticity. Not here some pastiche filled with overpriced bric-a-brac aimed at tourists; this was where many in the city did their daily shopping. Made up of more than a dozen separate markets, Aleppo's bazaar is still, as it was in the times of the Silk Road, the largest in the world and is said to be one of the best in the region. Each market specialises in a particular type of produce such as foodstuffs, cotton goods, jewellery or ironware, its unfathomable network of cobbled streets and passages criss-crossing a gently sloping hill under a roof of vaulted stonework and corrugated metal.

As I walked into the souk, I left behind the bright sunlight of the Levantine autumn and entered a world illuminated by a curious mix of electric bulbs, ornate lanterns and shafts of light falling through centuries-old oculi in the arched ceilings. Men and boys hurried about, transporting all manner of wares, faces glistening as they laboured to push hand trolleys piled high with heavy boxes and bulging sacks. Shoppers went about their business, buying, bargaining, arguing and joking while dark-haired youths sauntered arm in arm, pausing to chat with friends working on stalls, and women in headscarves perused packs of socks and bags of tea.

I saw more scarves in the souk in Aleppo than anywhere else I have ever been: stacked practically, draped seductively, hung demonstratively, they tempted even the most resolute to succumb to looking, even if not buying. The vendors were keen to convince me that half their stock was pashmina and, whenever I paused to look at their merchandise, hurriedly began unfolding one scarf after another, inviting me to feel the quality, not look at the width, or the Syrian equivalent thereof.

'Genuine pashmina!' I heard the stall owner proudly declare as I stopped to look at a particularly splendid example in blue and green. I looked up to see a titian-haired man smiling at me, his skin as pale as any European's. I felt the soft cloth between my fingers, its gentle fabric warm to the touch. He would make me a special price, he beamed, blue eyes twinkling. I wanted to ask him about his fair features, but feared he would consider me rude, so smiled and said I was just looking and that I might come back.

As I continued along the narrow passages, marvelling at the cornucopia of goods, a voice calling out behind me in Arabic gradually fought its way into my consciousness. Turning round, I had just enough time to leap out of the way of a tired-looking and rather grubby grey donkey on which sat an old man. A gnarled hand protruded from his beige *thobe*, fingers like polished twigs clutching tattered reins, but the scrawny beast seemed to know where it was going anyway. From under the off-white scarf draped over the man's head, I caught a glimpse of a face that could have been carved from the root of a tree. I watched as the strange pair turned and disappeared 'off stage' down one of the passages like extras from a play who have performed the same role for longer than anyone can remember.

Approaching a stand selling bathroom soaps and sponges, I saw a giant of a man deep in conversation with the young storekeeper, gesticulating with his hand, circling a finger as big as a sausage. Spotting me, his interlocutor held up a rectangular bar of dark green soap and waved me across. With his immaculately coiffed black hair and tanned skin, he resembled so many other men in this city; only a scar on his left temple made him stand out. Picking up another bar from the top of a pyramidal display surrounded by loofahs and dried starfish, he invited me to smell the hand-made soaps. With theatrical enthusiasm he held the bar to his face and sniffed deeply, eyes half closing as if momentarily transported to another, less mundane place.

I walked over and took the soap from his outstretched hand, trying not to look at his scar. A rough, square block, it had the unmistakeable fragrance of laurel. I realised it must be the famous Aleppo soap made from olive oil and reputed to have been used by beauties of antiquity such as Queen Zenobia of Palmyra and Cleopatra. I could feel the stallholder's eyes on me as I rubbed my fingers over the tablet with its calligraphy imprint. As if reading my mind, he assured me it was not expensive, yet of the finest quality.

His tall friend said something to him in Arabic. I looked up and saw he was an albino, his pale skin and startling pink eyes incongruous in this most oriental of environments. Only now did I notice wisps of white hair underneath the chequered dark blue scarf wrapped loosely round his head.

Eager to regain my attention, the soap seller began listing other perfumes: lavender, vanilla and cinnamon, and pointed enthusiastically to the stacks of soap. His albino friend had seen my surprise and now I was sure he sensed my embarrassment. I handed the bar back to its owner and asked how much it was.

'Two hundred,' he said, already wrapping it in brown paper.

The albino's pink eyes darted to his friend. However authentic the market was supposed to be, I suspected I had been quoted a tourist price, but did not want to haggle over a few cents. I handed over my Syrian pounds, took possession of my modest purchase and continued my exploration of the labyrinthine souk. I stopped to look at gleaming brassware and then drifted on as nonchalantly as possible as shopkeepers, ever on the alert for the slightest indication of interest, scuttled towards me like spiders whose web had been touched by a fly.

'Where are you from?' they called, but I just smiled in return, knowing that if I took the bait of answering a question I would be stuck in discussion for at least twenty minutes and that a friendly conversation would inevitably turn into an interminable sales pitch from which it would be difficult to escape. Then, as I approached a small crossroads of paths in the cotton souk, a boy, perhaps ten years old, scuttled past the rolls of brightly coloured fabric stacked against the stalls. It was his paper-white hair that caught my eye: he was another albino. I can count on one hand the number of albinos I have seen in my life, so to see two in one afternoon was extraordinary. I wondered if he was the son of the soap merchant's friend.

Eventually, the endless displays of clothing, household goods, dried foods and toiletries lost their charm and what had started out as an exotic feast for the eyes gradually metamorphosed into a prison of endless tunnels of polyester fabric and gaudy plastic. I decided to leave, but no matter which direction I took there seemed to be no way out, just more passages, more people, more hands holding out wares, and an endless chorus of sales pitches. As I remembered reading that the souk's passages ran to some thirteen kilometres, my chest started to feel tight with claustrophobia bordering on panic. Suddenly, I turned and saw daylight beyond a group of silhouettes drifting at the end of a passage. Once outside, I drank in the delicious autumn air before strolling, relieved, to the modern area of the city.

It was dusty and noisy, busy and, in parts, crowded. My throat was dry and the city air, which only moments ago had provided a welcome respite to the suffocating atmosphere of the bazaar, was now revealing itself as a warm, gaseous soup of exhaust fumes. I stopped for a drink at one of the pavement cafés and made myself comfortable on a plastic chair that had once been white. I watched the passers-by going about their daily business, carrying bags of shopping, talking to their children, rushing to appointments of which I knew nothing: I was an observer of life here, not an actor in it. The people I saw around me were the descendants of those who had inhabited the city in centuries past, of those who had conquered it, and of those who had passed through. As I sat sipping my iced mulberry juice or *sharab al toot*, I was struck that in the course of half an hour I had seen half a dozen red- or ginger-haired men. Even in Europe, I would not have expected to see so many. Perhaps the women of Aleppo also counted many redheads among their number, but, as most had their hair covered, it was impossible to be sure, although I thought it likely. After all, red hair is not gender-specific. I began to speculate as to the origin of the gene that was clearly so well established here and wondered if it were a trait left by the crusaders. Even if the Europeans had not managed to conquer the city, they had roamed the area, and no doubt sought to keep themselves amused. But, even more bizarrely, I saw another albino, a man in his thirties, his ghostlike features clearly visible from afar. As he came nearer, I tried not to stare: he had no way of knowing he was the third of his kind I had seen that day. Why there were so many in Aleppo was even more of a mystery than the origin of the city's redheads.

I decided to ask Nazim at the hotel. Seated at his desk in his small, simply furnished office he cut a handsome figure with his designer stubble, perfect smile and flawlessly ironed white shirt. The smile remained on his face, but, as I spoke, his eyes could not conceal a distinct change, an almost imperceptible transition from disconcerting to disingenuous. He twirled his pen in his hairy fingers while politely giving answers that had no bearing whatsoever on my questions, even when, thinking I had not been clear, I repeated them. Finally, putting the pen on the desk, he leant back in his chair, folded his hands in his lap and said he hoped I was enjoying my stay in the city. I was intrigued: there was no doubt about him having understood, but, clearly, he was not about to enlighten me.

The next day, I continued my exploration of the city, returning with almost masochistic curiosity to the sprawling souk. The second time round, it had an air of familiarity, the overbearing atmosphere of the day before having now evaporated. If I had tried to find him it would have been impossible to do so in the perplexing maze of passages, but, after wandering about for half an hour, I suddenly found myself just a few paces from the stall owned by the titian-haired scarf seller. His eyes lit up the moment he saw me. He greeted me as his friend and, rejoicing that I had returned, hurriedly reached for what he described as a 'beautiful, genuine pashmina scarf'.

Somewhat reluctantly, I walked across to where the happy salesman was busy unfurling an intricately patterned foulard in rich hues of burgundy, red and tan. He proudly flicked it over to reveal the reverse, giving repeated assurances of its quality. I examined it, not sensing any great urge to splash out and turning it this way and that with a hint of affected disdain. The scarf seller let it be known that he would make me a special price and asked how much I wanted to pay. As little as possible, I told him, not untruthfully. I put down the scarf and let my eyes wander indifferently to the curtains of others that lined the small stand. He asked me where I was from. Curiosity got the better of me. I decided to risk causing offence and asked him the same, saying that his blue eyes and red hair seemed unusual for the Middle East. He looked at me for a moment, evidently nonplussed, before saying he was from Aleppo, while he opened out another scarf and held it towards me.

Raising my eyebrows, I explained that he looked as if he was from Northern Europe and that I had been surprised by how many people I had seen in the city with red hair.

He glanced across to his dark-haired countryman on the stand diagonally opposite who, out of the corner of my eye, I could see was following our conversation with interest. He told me his hair colour was quite common in Syria, including in Damascus. When I countered that Arabs had dark hair, he said some people thought it came from the Kazakhs brought to the region many centuries ago as slaves. I speculated it might come from the crusaders, but he shrugged and did his best to turn my attention to a midnight blue and emerald scarf he was unfolding.

I preferred the first one and, after some gentle haggling, we agreed on a price. As the stallholder was folding my purchase and slipping it into a thin, blue plastic bag, I decided I would try once more and asked him about the albinos. For a moment, he did not react and seemed to be considering his answer. Then, handing me the bag, he said nobody knew where they were from, adding, after a brief pause, that they were special.

I said goodbye to the titian-haired stallholder, sensing he was relieved that the conversation was over and hearing as I walked away the man opposite say something to him in Arabic. I was now a proud owner of a smart scarf, as well as a bar of soap fit for a queen. Aleppo's souk might not be aimed at tourists, but, among all the everyday articles, there are still enough little gems for the visitor to discover.

I later read that the Mamluks who governed Aleppo in medieval times were, like the Kazakhs, originally brought as slaves, in their case from Circassia, a land in the Caucasus region. The Circassians were known for their red hair; indeed, in the fourteenth century a red-haired Mamluk even became Sultan of Cairo. Was my scarf seller a descendant of one of these slave warriors who rose to become a politically important caste, I wondered? Or did his origins perhaps lie with the crusaders after all? I contemplated what they would have thought had they known that the product of their loins would still be visible in the city centuries later. They failed to take the citadel, they failed to take the city, and their names are mostly forgotten, but could it be that in twenty-first-century Aleppo the genes of at least some of them are here for everyone to see?

As for the albinos, the puzzle remains. I have searched for clues about them, but to no avail. I have many memories of the city, including vivid recollections of the impressive citadel and the famous souk, but what has stayed in my mind most is the mystery of its white-haired inhabitants, carriers of a rare recessive gene. It seems nobody I know who has been to Aleppo has ever seen an albino there, let alone heard anything about their origin. Perhaps among those four hundred or so generations they could trace their genesis back to a single ancestor who, with his or her rare pigmentation, could well have been regarded with superstition or persecuted by their fellows. It is a strange immortality, but one that has outlived many of the grander attempts to be remembered by those who have passed through this city over the centuries.

Sunsets

The fisherman finished sorting the nets of the small wooden boat moored in the harbour, his bronzed skin covering the sort of lean muscle that comes only from many years' hard work. The heat of the Levantine day ebbed away as the sun drifted towards the horizon, turning the glistening sea copper and gold. To the east, sculpted hills basked in the last magical rays of the Canaanite sun goddess *Shapash* before slowly becoming silhouettes against the night sky. Oil lamps were starting to burn in the stone houses that lined the shore and bats fluttered, tiny shadows in the sky. Night would soon envelop the fisherman's world until *Shahar*, the god of dawn, summoned a new day and the dazzling orb rose again. Each morning, the fisherman took his boat out to sea whilst in the fields his neighbours tended their crops and in the market merchants sold wares brought on ships from lands across the water and from cities along the coast whose names he knew, but that he had never visited. Others laboured under the burning sun to load the same boats with prized cedar wood, fragrant source of the town's wealth, brought down from the mountains. Once done with his nets and boat, the fisherman would return to his modest home where his wife would be preparing a simple meal and tending to the children. In his world, the universe was created and ruled by a pantheon of gods whose representatives on Earth, the priests, determined how the fisherman and his fellow townsmen led their lives. The settlement in which he lived, with its sheltering harbour surrounded by fertile soils, had already been inhabited for thousands of years and, as far as he knew, life there had always been the same. Did he, as he cleaned his nets, ever think about the future, I wonder, or contemplate how his world, this city state on the coast, might look a few thousand years hence, just as at this very moment I am trying to imagine what it looked like when he lived here?

I am sitting on the remains of a stone wall that overlooks the sea, trying to envisage how Byblos appeared all those years ago. The fisherman of my imagination would scarcely recognise it today: only the sparkling Mediterranean and the outline of the hills behind me would be familiar. The rest, the mass of buildings pockmarking the countryside, the roads, the *autoroute*, would be bewildering; the cars, radios and mobile phones terrifying. And yet, as I contemplate the human life that has endured for millennia on this spot, I still feel there is a strong link to the past, that much of life here, when shorn of its modern trimmings and reduced to the essentials, is not so different from that of all those centuries ago. The small stone buildings nestling round the harbour, the quaint streets and the remains of the crusader castle perched on the little hill rising up from the shore bestow on Byblos a special atmosphere. Yet perhaps it is simply the timelessness of the sea itself that gives me the sensation of being more connected here to past worlds than in the great cities of the region for, despite their impressive buildings and illustrious histories, the metropolises of the Middle East are in many ways as modern as those anywhere. Even if everything else has changed, I know that the view of the sunset over the sea is one that I can share with my imaginary fisherman and that all the people who lived here in the course of a century of centuries also enjoyed.

As I sit on the warm stone looking out across the water, I reflect on the day that is drawing to a close. I drove up from Beirut late morning with Paco, the Spanish friend with whom I am staying and who has lived in Lebanon for several years. With his black hair and designer stubble, he could almost pass for Lebanese. He had seen an advert for the annual *Marché aux fleurs, oiseaux et produits traditionels* – the flower, bird and traditional products market – and thought it would make a nice day trip for us. Once out of the glittering chaos of the city itself and the usual logjam on the first few kilometres of road heading north, the traffic gradually thinned out. The *autoroute* wove its way along the rugged coastline, running past a landscape much of which was blighted by chaotic urban development. Virtually all of the country's famous cedar forests from which Byblos made its money had long since been felled. Eventually, the concrete gave way to more open views and I felt a flutter of pleasure at having left the oppidan sprawl behind. As we approached the turn off to Byblos, we passed a large roadside poster displaying a front-loading washing machine tied up with a huge red ribbon and, above it, the marketing slogan '*Give her something she really wants this Mother's Day*'. It was tempting to see it as ironic: indeed, at home, I could imagine it being used in a comedy sketch to lampoon attitudes from decades past, but here in Lebanon the message was serious, not humorous, and meant to denote generosity, not condescension. Something as banal as an advertisement for a domestic appliance spoke volumes about the society and its true level of economic development behind the polished façade.

We wandered around the old centre, compact and not without a certain magic, despite its touristic nature. The honey-coloured stone of which most of the old town is built exudes warmth and sets off the rich palette of greens provided by the exotic plants that cascade over the walls, and the palms and other trees that rise above the old medieval ramparts. Yet the juxtaposition is not merely of colour, but of texture and age, the rough, static stones standing solemnly whilst the luxuriant creepers and bougainvillea constantly regenerate and decorate the scene with flowers white and shocking pink. In this cramped and chaotic country, Byblos is a corner of Lebanon that is charming, picturesque and, for what is a pushy and ruthless nation, incongruously romantic. You might want to party with Beirut, but it is Byblos you should marry.

Like so many places in the region, this town has, over the course of time, been known by various names. It was the Ancient Greeks who dubbed it *Byblos*, the term they also gave to papyrus as so much of it was shipped from here; the Greek *biblion*, meaning book, has the same origin and gave us the word Bible. Today, the road signs mark Byblos as Jbeil, an Arabic word derived from the Canaanite Gebal.

We stopped for a drink at one of the cafés that line the pedestrianised area of the old centre and spent a while watching the world go by. As Paco recounted an anecdote about his evacuation by the French navy during the Israeli bombardment of 2006, I found my attention unwittingly caught by the *beau monde* strolling past, chatting and explaining, discussing and gesturing. How long, I wondered, had the women spent applying their make-up and doing their hair to perfect the magazine-cover look? And how many weeks, months, years had the men worked out to acquire the V-shaped torsos that were squeezed into body-hugging T-shirts? I smiled inwardly at their devotion to the aesthetic: modesty is an alien concept in this country. The people are proud of their roots as Phoenicians, the name bestowed by the Greeks on the renowned seafarers and traders of ancient Canaan, whose sharp business skills have been passed down throughout the generations and now seem to be almost a genetic trait of every Lebanese.

'*Oye, guapo*, are you listening to me?' laughed Paco, poking me firmly on the arm.

'Of course,' I replied, only half truthfully. 'There is just so much to see here.'

Opposite the café, the modest dimensions of the Place de l'Unesco had been given over to the colourful market. Potted and bedding plants were set out on the stone paving in table-sized rectangles, some shaded from the sun by large white parasols. With Mother's Day less than twenty-four hours away, the timing was perfect. People milled along the pathways between the densely-packed rows of tulips, pansies, begonias and hydrangeas, surveying the specimens. A *dame d'un certain âge*, elegant in perfectly pressed slacks, a light pullover draped over her bony shoulders, tried to retain her husband's attention while she discussed a parlour palm, her jewellery glistening in the sun as she gently examined the fronds. A little further on, a young couple carefully picked out geraniums while their two small children squabbled over a teddy bear. Paco and I finished our coffees and meandered over to the little market to take a closer look. The scent of rosemary and lavender danced alongside heady oriental perfumes and cigarette smoke, while Arabic and French wove together seamlessly in the conversations around us. An earnest-looking young man behind a table with jars of honey and sachets of dried herbs was talking to a woman as she inspected one of the pots. I wondered if he realised that his polo shirt was almost Tyrian purple, the colour of the dye obtained from sea snails, once worth its weight in silver and from which his ancestors made their fortune supplying the elites of Greece and Rome. He looked at us as we walked past, his face warming with a familiar smile, his regard lingering a moment too long. We made our way slowly round the market till we came to a stall set up with oil paintings of local scenes and buildings like those around us. A portrait of an old woman, seemingly local and cheerful in her beige headscarf, looked copied from a photograph. The forty-something artist, in white shirt and jeans, hovered by the canvases with contrived indifference, his dark sunglasses veiling his true thoughts. We paused to look at the limited collection before continuing, casually, on our way.

Paco suggested we go to the souk and, taking my arm, led me through a stone passageway that opened out onto a carefully renovated street lined with single-storey shops. The souk looked more like a stage set than a traditional Middle Eastern bazaar: spotless paving stones and decorative cobbles ran between the two rows of improbably tidy shops with old-fashioned lanterns hanging from their wide eaves. We walked up one side and back down the other, perusing the souvenirs: postcards, Lebanese flags, mugs, rainbow windmills for children and the ubiquitous scarves in any colour one could think of. Stopping to inspect a display of watercolours of the harbour and town, Paco asked me if I wanted to buy anything. I shook my head and smiled. We walked on, briefly entering a bookshop and a dimly-lit store peddling a few tatty and overpriced lithographs of local scenes, nothing I felt compelled to add to my modest collection back home. Our last stop was a place selling fossils – fishes and shrimps caught forever in slices of stone. It seemed a strange spot for such a shop, its ancient rocks a stark contrast to the touristic junk for sale elsewhere in the street. Ironically for a town once one of the great commercial centres of the world, today Byblos' souk is a souk only in name, a mere pastiche through which urbane Beirutis and cautious tourists can wander without worrying about the risk of seeing anything real.

Before long, we reached the end and, strolling through another covered passageway, found ourselves in a small square with a patch of emerald green grass in its centre. A short distance away to the south, the twelfth-century crusader castle stood on a modest rise, its thick walls designed to keep out attackers now but a cultural highlight for sightseers. Yet, despite its impressive ramparts and imposing castle, Giblet, as the Crusaders called Byblos, fell first in 1187 to Saladin, Sultan of Egypt and Syria, and then to the warrior-sultan Baybars less than a century later, just two of the many invasions and conquests the town has seen since it was first settled in Neolithic times. We headed towards the citadel and the entrance to the archaeological site, beyond which lay the ruins of millennia of human occupation.

A row of half a dozen pillars, resurrected from among the dust and scraggy oleander bushes and topped with eroded Corinthian capitals, are among the few substantial remains of what was once ancient Byblos. It was here, over 3,500 years ago, that the Phoenicians, needing to keep track of all the goods they traded, invented the first *abjad* or consonant-based alphabet. All Western alphabets are derived from their creation. The first two letters represented 'ox' and 'house' respectively, which, when translated into Greek, evolved to become alpha and beta. The original Phoenician '*aleph*' is still today the name of the first letter of the Hebrew alphabet and, of course, beta lives on in both the Arabic and Hebrew words for house, '*beit*'. That this relatively little-known town is the source of one of the most basic elements of our modern world is testified to by UNESCO registering the Phoenician alphabet as part of the documentary heritage of humankind, its importance transcending the boundaries of time and culture.

As we wandered between the low walls and random stones, I found it difficult to imagine how the place must have looked in antiquity. Where once high priests had made offerings and young wives had baked bread, gently lilting grass and meadow flowers now grew; where before sweating soldiers had marched and wily merchants had haggled over prices, today thorny shrubs and verdant palms held sway. Ironically, if nowadays the inhabitants of yore would scarcely be able to identify the ruins of their town's once impressive stone buildings, they would probably recognise the delicate yellow and white blooms that soak up the sun. The lavish public architecture of this once great trading town had proven less enduring than the fragile flowers of the field. I paused to sit on a round stone, perhaps the vestiges of a column from a magnificent palace, and looked out at the Mediterranean, its waters sparkling in the spring sunshine. I watched Paco's slight figure as he wandered slowly across the site, his thoughts elsewhere. The Phoenicians settled in his country, too: his distant ancestors might once have trodden the same path along which he now picked his way, texting a message in an alphabet that had its origins in this very place.

After a while, we returned to the square in front of the castle before walking through another passageway in the thick medieval fortifications. We emerged to find ourselves in a sloping alley lined on both sides with thin, upright willows growing so close to the rough walls as to be touching them and forming an arched canopy of gentle branches, wispy fingers diffusing the sunlight that fell on to the path.

Soon, we reached the harbour where a rather decrepit collection of fishing vessels, speed boats and pocket-sized pleasure cruisers bobbed languorously in the murky water, a sad reminder of Byblos' 1960s heyday when, fleetingly, the town was a favourite of glamorous film stars. Now, peeling paint, frayed flags and oily water were the order of the day. On the north side of the waterfront, a trio of half-empty restaurant terraces, including one styling itself as '*le rendezvous des personalités internationales*', was perched above stone retaining walls, the few diners there showing little interest in the harbour view below. We continued past parked cars to the breakwater and joined families and teenagers ambling along the broad concrete walkway to the end. Groups of young boys, tanned and slim, sat on the rocks, chatting, throwing pebbles into the sea or shouting encouragement to those who had ventured into the water to join the plastic bottles and other flotsam that drifted with the current. I wondered if they ever reflected on their town's long history or thought about their ancestors: great kings such as Ahirom, whose name was literally carved in stone on his sarcophagus, now in the National Museum of Beirut, and countless others whose lives went unrecorded and who returned to dust to be forever forgotten.

We walked back around the harbour and entered the few lanes that make up the old part of Byblos, traditional stone houses occasionally interspersed by a modern villa with a perfect sea view. As the land rose behind the harbour, streets were replaced by pathways and, in just a few paces, we found ourselves in a less manicured world where the small homes seemed to be locked in an existential struggle with the thick vegetation that grew all around them. Twisted fig trees and windblown palms were joined by gangs of weeds and tangled bushes that crept between walls and silently gripped wrought iron gates as if determined to reclaim the core of this ancient town. Renovated, the buildings could have been quaint, but as it was they were merely dilapidated and sad. Seeing a narrow flight of stone steps lead off between two walls, we headed up them, brushing away the insects and flies that dropped off the overhanging leaves and branches as we pushed our way past, for a moment schoolboys once more. After a few steps turning this way and that, we found ourselves on a grassy platform overlooking the sea painted with the first lines of copper and auburn as the sun began drifting towards the horizon. In silence, we watched as a small boat slowly sailed towards the harbour.

Behind us, on the other side of the path, a dense patch of low vegetation covered the ground between the grass and a crumbling stone wall. At first, it seemed to be nothing more than more weeds, but then I recognised the familiar shapes of parsley, chives, sage and other herbs thriving in the cool half-shadow of a nearby tree. As soon as I realised what they were, I suddenly became aware of their fragrances floating around us, mingling with a faint smell of rosemary I had already noticed.

A voice broke into the early evening air. We looked round to see an old woman, a housecoat over her simple clothes, slippers on her feet, slowly making her way towards us. Only now did I notice a few garments hanging limply from a washing line a short distance away and realise that the run-down buildings beyond them were occupied: we had strayed into her garden. She spoke again, her guttural Arabic tones unintelligible to me, but the timbre discernibly friendly. Her gait was uncertain, her thin legs supporting a lean body, perhaps a deflated version of her former self. Apparently undeterred by the lack of response, she continued her monologue. I apologised in English and then in French for trespassing, but she did not react; instead she bent down and began tearing at the plants. I tried to catch Paco's eye, but his regard was focused on the old woman. Straightening up and still speaking, she held out a handful of basil as if it were a posy and nodded for me to take it. Surprised, I hesitated before reaching out and taking the small gift from her hand, rough from years of hard work and burnt almost to the colour of leather by the eternal sun. I expected her dark eyes to glisten with kindness, but they were just weary and dull.

'*Shukran*,' I mumbled, repeating my thanks more loudly as the old woman turned away.

She continued her soliloquy, making a sweeping movement with a thin arm in the direction of the harbour below. I was unsure whether she was speaking to us or to herself, but endeavoured to look as if I were listening. The tone of her voice recounted a tale of better days, infused perhaps with regret and nostalgia for a time when her hair was sable rather than silver. After a while, she seemed to tire and bid us what I assumed to be a farewell.

'*Au revoir, et merci*,' I called as she walked slowly back along the path.

'*Allah yasalmik*,' said Paco, who had listened discreetly but not reacted to the old woman's ramblings. He turned to look at me and shrugged his shoulders, his intensely blue eyes as bright as ever despite the fading light.

I contemplated the basil and then the herb garden before turning to follow the path a short distance where another, wider flight of stone steps led further up the hill. Unkempt, dishevelled, this seemingly forgotten part of town was beyond the route most tourists chose.

'What did she say?' I asked Paco, a couple of paces behind me, as I passed an upturned plastic chair in a tiny, overrun garden that had known better times.

'What everyone of her generation here says,' he sighed after a pause.

At the top of the steps the path continued a few paces before broadening out into a lane. The overgrown world of the hillside melted away and once again we were in a carefully maintained street.

Ahead of us loomed a small square building; a modest dome on top and a couple of arches attached to its side looked more like afterthoughts than an integral part of a planned design. A petite bell tower rising from the flat roof added a delicate touch to an otherwise squat, solid-looking structure, the tiny cross atop it standing out against the startlingly azure sky. Its masonry was of the same rough stone as most of the old buildings in Byblos, yet it stood surrounded by paving that evoked a modern art interpretation of a chess board. High up, bunches of greenery clung to the stonework as if seeking sanctuary, their dainty flowers out of reach of those who would pick them as an ephemeral souvenir, only to discard them hours later. Even so, the small windows, set at various heights in the thick walls, gave it more the aspect of a tiny castle than the Romanesque-style church it was. As we arrived at the twelfth-century building named after St John the Baptist, we were not alone: men in sharp black suits and women in haute couture mingled around the entrance, oblivious to passers-by. It could have been a fashion show, it could have been a film set, or it could have been a wedding: in Lebanon, it seems that even the participants are not always sure.

We ambled on and eventually found ourselves back at the market. It was busier than when we had first walked round it, but there seemed to be just as many flowers and plants. From a row of little cages filled with canaries and finches birdsong floated through the early evening air. We contemplated cacti and perused plumbago, our pace determined by the shuffling mass of day-trippers who now filled the square. Suddenly, I realised I was gazing at jars of honey of the deepest amber and, looking up, saw the young man we had noticed before. He was perhaps in his early twenties and somewhat slimmer than the average Lebanese male, whose body is given form by military service and further honed in the gym. He smiled shyly as if suppressing a firmer emotion. Paco took a jar of honey in his slender fingers and, giving it a cursory examination, began to speak to him in Arabic. The tone was matter-of-fact, but my friend is a poet and I knew his words would be carefully chosen and elegant. The young man laughed nervously, white teeth flashing. Paco spoke again and, after hesitating, the young man nodded. The transaction was executed quickly and we walked away, my host now the owner of a jar of finest Lebanese honey, apparently produced by bees that live among the country's few remaining cedar trees. The day was drawing to a close and the market would soon be over. I told Paco I would like to watch the sun go down.

The orange disc has almost reached the horizon and is about to slip into the sea and into the underworld beyond, guided by *Shalim*, the god of dusk. This small town has outlived many of its great contemporaries: Palmyra, Ur, Babylon and Uruk lie in ruins, their erstwhile grandeur of legend now nothing more than bare stones and crumbling mounds. The buildings in Byblos, which once stood coevally with the fine architecture of such cities, are now also reduced to mere relics, but, in contrast to the others, Byblos itself has survived. Like the plants adorning the town's ramparts and the flowers among the ruins, it has constantly renewed itself, retaining an alluring youthfulness and flourishing centuries after others have faded into the desert. Over time, hundreds of generations have enjoyed the splendour of the setting sun from this spot, including the fisherman of my daydreams. Illiterate he might have been, his life uncomplicated by today's comforts and technology, but he would still have been able to take pleasure in the beauty of the day's end. Although separated by millennia and our understanding of the event, it was an experience we shared: it was his sunset and it was mine.

My thoughts drift on the warm evening air to the old woman in her cottage. The ascetic lifestyle I envisage her leading might not be so different from that of my imaginary fisherman of antiquity. I look at the wilting spray of basil, the herb that represents best wishes, and wonder if anyone will buy her a Mother's Day gift. Perhaps a washing machine. Somehow, I doubt it. But maybe the glow of tomorrow's sunset will bring her a few moments of familiar joy.

In the City of Sinbad
– Fortune and Fate

I am sitting on a yellow plastic chair looking at an unloaded handgun and reflecting on the day's events. The evening air is warm and the chatter in the background lends a sense of the ordinary to a world that is anything but. I consider myself lucky to be here, but even luckier to be able to leave.

Like some slain monster the capsized ship lay motionless on its side, the murky waters lapping against its rusting hull. Where once white paint had gleamed, corroding metal now crumbled away, flake by flake, while the last vestiges of wooden decking clung precariously to the vertical. Two bearded fishermen crouched near the stern on what might previously have been the wall of the ship's bridge; a third, wearing a khaki-green bucket hat, sat on a curved piece of brown metal, the stump of a missing leg tucked underneath his light grey *thobe*. The trio watched as we sailed slowly past, their fishing lines hanging limply, faces expressionless. The ship, blown out of the water by fighter planes during the Iraq war, was now a rotting carcass, just one more ugly scar left by the bloody conflict that flashed onto television screens around the world in the early years of this century. Since the war ended, media interest has gradually faded and the public in the West has enjoyed the luxury of boredom setting in as post-conflict violence drags on over the years. For the people of Basra, however, the aftermath is still visible and, even if the television crews have long since packed their bags and left, the consequences of the invasion continue to unfold, inexorably changing the culture and life of the city.

We cruised on in our little boat towards the metal pontoon bridge that spans the Shatt al-Arab – the Stream of the Arabs – the broad waterway formed by the confluence of the Tigris and Euphrates. A line of cars and minibuses, many going to or from the border with Iran just a few kilometres away, clanked and clunked their way slowly over the temporary link. The boatman, a lean figure with chestnut-coloured skin, steered a course under a gap at the side where the bridge rose to meet the riverbank. We continued across the rippling grey water, the zephyr created as we sailed ahead providing a welcome, if small, relief from the otherwise muggy air.

Eventually, we came alongside a large motor yacht moored on the right bank. In better condition it could have been the sort of boat a Russian oligarch would keep in Antibes or Monaco, but the erstwhile polar-white paintwork was now grubby, as if starting to take on the colour of the river. Around the waterline it was beginning to peel away in the humid heat, revealing dark rust below. A funnel and a fading stripe along the boat's side, both cobalt blue, were the only concessions to colour on the sober exterior, but we knew that, inside, the vessel had been extravagantly decorated with arabesque opulence. Not a soul was to be seen on deck, the yacht's windows a corpse's lifeless eyes. The pitch of our small engine dropped as we slowed down before passing along the length of the dormant ship. Staring at the silent vessel, I tried to imagine how different life on board must have been in the past. Eventually, we reached the square stern where the name *BASRA BREEZE* was painted in large capital letters. The superyacht, previously Saddam Hussein's floating palace, now lay silently awaiting a buyer, a dictator's widow seeking a new husband. Captain Hassan and Sergeant Ahmed, the plain-clothes guards from the Ministry of the

Interior, took photographs as eagerly as would any tourist. Omar, the forty-something guide and interpreter sitting with his arms outstretched along the sides of the boat, had obviously seen it all before. In his limited English, Hassan asked me if I liked it; I returned his smile and said I did. The joviality of the two men made it easy to slip into a false sense of security, but, behind their gum-chewing, laid-back style, I knew they were carefully watching everything around us.

The boatman revved up the engine and we moved on. With one bony hand on the tiller, he used the other to adjust the black and white chequered scarf that was balanced on his head like a loose turban. My thoughts drifted to the legendary Sinbad whom I imagined sailing along the same waterway as he set off on his adventures from Basra, his home town. In those days, it was a major centre of culture and learning that had grown out of a military encampment founded by the second caliph, Umar Ibn al Khattab, the man whose conquests spread Islam across vast swathes of the Middle East. Surely Sinbad had enjoyed a more uplifting view, I thought. In the course of his seven voyages, the intrepid seafarer encountered many perils and endured much suffering, but, in the end, he became fabulously rich. Now, ahead of us, evidence of latter-day wealth was looming into view, yet the collection of two-storey sandy-pink bunkers, their roofs as flat as the surrounding landscape, was not my idea of a palace. Weary palms, browning fronds hanging from lopsided crowns, and flowing pistachio trees softened the angular design of the low buildings, but could do little to beautify what were essentially unsightly concrete boxes covered by a veneer of rose-coloured stone. Ali, the young photographer mysteriously sent by the Ministry of Tourism to accompany us for part of the trip, lifted the weighty camera that hung on a strap round his thin neck and began snapping picture after picture. A native of Baghdad, it was his first trip to the south of the country and Basra.

Although he tried not to show it, he was evidently excited and regularly asked Hassan to take a photograph of him standing in front of the historical sites and mosques we visited. His fingers, unusually elegant for a man's, grappled with the focus while he pointed the camera towards the shore. A few figures wandered around the broad balconies and behind the rolls of barbed wire and sandbags that surrounded the abandoned residence. Here, in days gone by, Saddam and his family had surrounded themselves with dictator kitsch and enjoyed pleasures beyond the wildest dreams of those they ruled. Like the famous Saladin, he was a native of Tikrit, but, unlike the sultan who died leaving only one gold coin and forty seven pieces of silver, Saddam did not give his money to the poor. And yet for all the wealth he amassed, the former leader of Iraq who, from the terraces of this unsightly edifice, once cast his gaze over his dominions, ended up seeking refuge in a hole in the ground near his birthplace.

I took a last look at the dingy palace and then we turned round to head back. We cut a wide semi-circle in the river and sailed on past dusty fields and stony beaches strewn with litter. A group of feral dogs ran along the top of the bank that rose just a couple of metres above the shoreline. They paused to sniff at something, then trotted inland towards a mass of straggly bushes where they disappeared from view. I watched as we passed occasional buildings and huts at the edges of the fields, eerily empty, the palm trees behind them little more than silhouettes in the haze. A small sphere glowed white behind the grey cloud that covered what should have been a sunny land. As we made our way back to Basra, a narrow, wooden boat spluttered past, clouds of white smoke billowing from its stern, its wake spanning out until it gently rocked our vessel. With its yellow canvas roof and old tyres hung along its sides, it seemed like the twin of our own little craft. I looked at the handful of passengers huddled along its gunwales. The men were all in white, the women completely in black; they could have been borrowed from a human chess set. In another time perhaps: board games, such as the once popular backgammon, are now frowned upon by the increasingly religious establishment in Southern Iraq. As the buildings and trees disappeared from sight, the view became one of overwhelming greyness, as if the water and sky had given up being blue and instead sunk into some sort of cosmic depression. It was strangely appropriate for the setting and I tried to determine if the dullness created the gloom or merely reflected it. Only the river bank, a horizontal band of green topped with sandy earth broke the monotone, its edges blurred against the opaque sky.

A while later, we passed back under the pontoon bridge and headed towards our mooring place. Slowing down, we chugged past a forest of broken wooden pilings that rose from the water's edge like rotting, black teeth. Between them lay pieces of rusting machinery, chunks of concrete and abandoned digging equipment, scattered like a child's toys as if the city had been subjected to a visitation by a rampaging giant. Just a few paces behind this impromptu junk-yard stood a run-down fairground where a Ferris wheel was gently turning, even though most of its thirty or so brightly painted cabins were empty.

We sailed on to the mouth of the creek and the small landing stage from where we had set off. A group of young boys in grubby, ill-fitting clothes watched with curiosity as our boat drew up, the battered tyres along its side breaking the impact when we finally came to a standstill beside the quay. As we clambered out, an Iraqi family was waiting to board after us. The father, a middle-aged man whose light-blue shirt stretched over his paunch, stood in front of his wife and teenage daughter, each of whom was wrapped in a black polyester *abaya*. I caught a glimpse of denim touching a golden sandal and imagined the suffocating heat beneath the sticky fabric. Three small boys in Western clothing, hair cropped short, and their younger sister, no more than six or seven years old, followed closely behind. She, too, was in an *abaya*, her wide eyes staring out from a face surrounded by black cloth. Not for the first time in this country, I saw a child covered in a robe intended to temper the libido of any men who saw her and found myself trying to understand why she should need to wear such a thing.

We began walking towards Lion of Babylon Square, along the way passing buildings that resembled a jumble of cardboard boxes tied together by the network of cables criss-crossing between them. A few billboards advertising washing powder and telecoms brightened up the place, but men in dark suits staring out from rows of political posters were an omnipresent reminder of the fragile political situation. The faces were trying to look friendly, reassuring, but their only saving grace in this increasingly intolerant country was that they did not have long beards and were not wearing turbans. We made our way towards the entrance to the souk and an open-air market in front of it that had been set up between a couple of rows of parked vehicles. I could see people wandering about. From a distance, those draped in black looked like gaps in the scene before us, shapes of *personae non gratae* cut out of a photograph. The Iranian influence was seeping over the border like an oil slick, contaminating all it touched, covering women in black as crude clings to seabirds. The market itself was a sad display of cheap Chinese goods in flimsy boxes, with plastic toys, batteries and disposable lighters laid out on sheets placed over the uneven ground. I felt I had entered a parallel universe, a world in which the people around me were trapped, but from which I could walk away.

We headed into the souk, swapping daylight for the glow of economy bulbs. I knew Hassan and Ahmed, one in front of us and one behind, were keeping a discreet lookout for any sign of trouble as they sauntered past the stalls. The souk was a jumble of colours and textiles: polo tops, *thobes*, shirts and *abayas* filled the walls and shelves of the tiny shops from floor to ceiling and hung from the roof of the aisles between them, a dense kaleidoscope of oversized bunting. In a country where so many people have lost limbs through conflict and terrorist attacks, it was disconcerting to see legs of mannequins hanging among the pendent clothes, a thoughtless reminder of what had been so brutally taken away. Wherever the passages were wide enough, tables had been set up and covered with packets of socks, T-shirts and men's underwear. Storeholders chatted, shoppers inspected goods, the guards kept an eye out and, of course, people stared.

As we ventured deeper into the souk, the crowds thinned out and there was more space between the little stores, providing us with glimpses of older walls. Even so, it was a far cry from the exotic markets I had seen elsewhere in the region and a world away from the Basra of *Tales from the Thousand and One Nights*. At the far end of the bazaar, there were a few stalls selling army and police surplus. Ahmed examined a pair of desert boots, turning them over to look at the grip, a stark contrast to his own smooth-soled, pointed shoes. Laughing, he said something to Hassan before putting them back. For a brief moment, I pondered how an entire uniform might be fun for fancy dress parties, but then, with a sense of unease, realised how simple it would be for anyone to disguise himself as a representative of the very forces of law and order that had accompanied us throughout the trip.

I was standing in the old Jewish quarter. The haze was starting to lift and the sun beginning to glare down on us pitilessly, as if determined to compensate for its earlier absence. With its canals and fine architecture, Basra had once been known as the Venice of the East. The narrow channel in front of me, though, bordered with one-time magnificent merchants' houses, was now a stagnant waterway filled with garbage, its thick stench pervading the ever warmer spring air. The houses themselves, now perhaps no more than half a dozen or so, were crumbling, their beige bricks holding together as a man who feels it is too early to die clings to life. The occasional window pane or insert of tiles the colour of lapis lazuli brightened up otherwise dull façades while ornate brickwork decorations around windows and doorways recalled better times. Above me, dark wooden balconies and *mashrabiyas*, the bay windows typical of Arab city houses, spoke of a distant era when – relatively speaking – lives could be lived without fear. I looked at the rickety structures with sun-bleached traces of turquoise clinging to the splintering wood and their weathered slats hanging like broken wings. Once upon a time, from behind the privacy of the latticework, the houses' inhabitants would have been able to observe the goings-on in the street below. As the residents watched the world outside, the updraft created by the sun heating the dark wood of the *mashrabiya* would have drawn the heat out of the adjacent rooms, in turn sucking cooler air from the cellar to provide a gentle but refreshing draft for those indoors. It was a simple but effective system and one that worked with the environment rather than against it.

A small group of policemen in flak jackets, automatic weapons at the ready, hung about guarding us while we looked at the sad remnants of what had been a thriving and wealthy area. Omar led us to one of the crumbling two-storey houses. '*Ministry of Culture*' and '*Basrah Museum*' (sic), said the board outside. The arched windows, reaching almost to the ground, had bars on them, but the front door, battered and dirty, stood ajar. We stepped over the stone doorsill, concave from wear, and down into the dim entrance hall, my eyes taking a moment or two to adjust. A musty smell seeped out from the shadows on either side while ahead, from between decrepit walls, sunlight pierced a gap beyond which a thin column of green was just visible. At first, I thought the building was abandoned, but, as we walked around, I gradually realised that there were desks and chairs in the dusty and decaying interior. The rooms were more like empty offices than a museum. Scattered on tiled floors were dust-covered sheets of cardboard and empty plastic water bottles. As I entered one of the rooms, a skinny black and white cat scampered away; it paused to turn and watch me for a moment and then dashed through a doorway at the far end.

I headed towards the sunlight and picked my way into what had previously been the garden. A couple of large trees were poised valiantly in a last stand; around them, three or four scraggy date palms and creepers and other plants, deprived of care, had already reverted to their wild state in an effort to survive. A lanky oleander bush that had managed to produce a few pink flowers swayed gently, and delicate notes of birdsong drifted on the warm breeze. Suddenly, the *adhan* began and the almost bucolic atmosphere of the overgrown garden melted away in an instant. The voice of the muezzin floated across the air from a loudspeaker, sounding unusually melodic as if being sung rather than simply called out. I turned and saw Omar, arms folded, watching me through the open windows of the wooden façade that ran the length of the first floor. I smiled and waved a hand in acknowledgement. Looking at the delicate patterns of geometric shapes cut into the panels around the window frames, I wondered how the artisans who had toiled to produce such beauty would feel if they could see the state of their labours now.

Back inside, Hassan and Ahmed were wandering around the decaying building with an air of mild curiosity and Ali was busy taking photographs. Cautiously, we made our way up the creaking stairs; I half expected them to collapse at any moment and send us crashing below in a cloud of dust. We paused on the first floor, where Omar was hovering at the end of the corridor. The light from the open windows shone past his half-silhouetted figure onto the black and white tiled floor and crumbling plaster of the wall opposite. Specks of dust floated lazily in the heat of the afternoon and for a moment an incongruous serenity seemed to descend like some invisible gossamer. A floorboard squeaked and the feeling was gone. We moved on. There were more empty offices, unswept floorboards, peeling paintwork and, above all this, mahogany-coloured ceilings bordered by gold-painted inlay and carvings. Looking at the craftsmanship, I wondered if peace and stability would ever arrive in time to save these wonderful Ottoman houses. Sadly, I felt I knew the answer. I walked over to one of the *mashrabiyas* and peered through the wooden slats. Down on the street, two of the policemen were enjoying a cigarette and talking. I reflected on how many of their direct colleagues might have been killed or maimed at the hands of those who have no interest in seeing a stable society here. Were these men brave, dedicated, or simply desperate for a job? As I watched them, a little girl with an ebony plait and a long raspberry-pink and blue dress scuttled past clutching a bag of crisps, undaunted by the heavy weaponry within arm's reach.

We continued up the stairs and emerged on to the flat roof. Covered with terracotta floor tiles and bordered by a low wall, it must once have been a pleasant place to sit on a summer's evening and watch the stars. Today, the view across the low-rise city was a patchwork of sandy-coloured bricks, breeze blocks, corrugated iron and concrete, linked by cables and wires. Bouquets of green protruded here and there, and lines of washing added an occasional touch of colour. An Iraqi flag wafted from a pole at the front, while the sun, no longer a veiled white disc, beat down, the polluted haze above the city no match for its full fury.

Back on the street, we crossed a small bridge that spanned the fetid canal and walked over to another dilapidated house. The double front doors, their ageing wood holding out despite obvious neglect, swung open. A tall man in his sixties appeared on the threshold and, apparently expecting us, straight away bade us enter. As we filed in, he ushered us along a short hallway to a square atrium where three elderly men were lingering. All rather short and stout, there was a distinct similarity between them. Small, rodent eyes peered out from above large noses as they watched us like children who had been told to be on their best behaviour. They nodded greetings and gave nicotine smiles before deferentially stepping back, fading away. A row of four low, black vinyl sofas, presumably reserved for dignitaries, faced a large desk at the front of the atrium. Behind them, stood half a dozen rows of chairs, their covers tattered and torn. With a sweep of a hand, a smile and a few words of Arabic, our host invited us to look around. I was not quite sure what I was supposed to be looking at, but stepped forward. The whole atrium was bathed in a bluish-green luminosity. It seemed to be coming from the sunlight reflecting off sea-green pillars that supported a mezzanine and the lapis lazuli blue of the wooden ceiling bordering the glass roof high above. Behind the desk, a white-haired man looked out from a large poster on the wall above which a banner read 'the union of basrah writers' (sic). In the eighth and ninth centuries, the city had been a great cultural centre where poets, men of letters and religious scholars had once thrived; one of its governors had even built a library of 15,000 books. Now, it seemed, Basra's literary heritage was involved in the same existential struggle as its architectural.

Suddenly, Mozart's *Eine kleine Nachtmusik* filled the air, pouring at full volume from a pair of speakers near a desk where our host stood beaming. His posture and perfectly pressed grey shirt and trousers lent him a military aspect, diminished only by his artistically long silver hair. While the music blared out, I perused the posters that adorned the walls: huge photographs of writers I had never heard of sporting 1970s moustaches and faded advertisements for artistic events long past. Pointing to the upstairs, I asked one of the ageing trio hovering about if I could go up, hoping my sign language would be understood, even if English were not. He looked at me for a moment, nodded and, with a shake of a hand, indicated a doorway.

I began exploring the various rooms that led off the square mezzanine like prison cells, peering through the arched doors to find piles of books and papers on the floor, cardboard boxes and broken chairs, all covered in a thick layer of dust: the efforts to maintain a degree of normality on the ground floor had not extended to the upper storey. Returning to the balcony, I looked over the balustrade at the space below where the policemen in their light beige trousers and dark blue polo shirts were milling around, weapons hanging limply at their sides. Ali was wandering about, adjusting the strap on his camera in between taking pictures of the atrium. Just twenty-four, he was keen to practise his limited English, often sitting next to me as our little group drove around. He took every opportunity to ask me questions and check vocabulary, mostly through improvised sign language. He saw me and grinned, before raising his dark eyebrows, shrugging his shoulders and pointing upstairs. The music changed abruptly to Beethoven's *Für Elise* and a small bird, apparently trapped inside the building, flew up towards the glass roof, its chirping scarcely audible above the noise. I watched Ali as he quickly tried to photograph it and wondered what relevance the picture could have to his assignment.

Back downstairs, Omar was talking to the man who had let us in and who was looking pensive and nodding. He saw me and beckoned me across.

'*Il parle français,*' he said.

'*Oui, oui!*' smiled our host, ever nameless.

In the brief conversation that followed, I learnt, if the surroundings did not already make the point clear, that being an intellectual and writer in current day Iraq was not easy. Unsure what I was expected to say, I nodded sympathetically before concluding the exchange with a smile and drifting away. In the strange blue-green light one of the policemen, an improbably rakish scarf tied under his shirt collar, was reading a poster, two others were casually talking and the three old men were loitering impatiently. The piano music, the blurred strains of which had been echoing round the atrium, stopped only to be immediately replaced by blasts of the *March of the Toreadors* from Carmen. As if on cue, everyone headed towards the exit, the policemen once again bringing their guns into position.

Moments later, we were back out in the hot Mesopotamian sun, the old wooden door clicking shut behind us. The writers' union had felt like an outpost struggling to maintain the last vestiges of secular culture, especially any with a hint of the West, in a city coming increasingly under the shadow of its neighbour. One could ask whether it matters if, in the city of Sinbad, there is cultural space for the music of eighteenth-century Austrian composers, or writers who speak French, yet, as I was to find out, it is not just Hesperian culture that is being driven out of Basra, but anyone and anything that does not conform to the worldview of the extremists.

We were sitting in a long, air-conditioned room a good half-hour drive from the Jewish quarter. Hassan and Ahmed were opposite me, ensconced in two of the heavy wooden chairs that lined the marble walls, busy looking at the Captain's camera and the pictures he had taken earlier on. Only now did I notice that the Sergeant had not shaved today, a dense designer stubble having formed round his chubby features. Sunglasses tucked into the breast pocket of his shirt, he pointed a thick finger at the display on the camera with a comment that made his boss laugh. Hassan saw me watching and smiled with a cheeky glint in his eye. Above, a flotilla of glass chandeliers, each shaped like a three-sailed boat on a round, twinkling sea, hung from the peach-coloured ceiling. My eyes wandered to an alcove at the far end of the room where a cross made of logs was draped with a tasselled shroud. The entire symbol was a *bas-relief*. In parts the white plaster cerement merged seamlessly with the wall on which six olive branches had been painted protruding from the cross. On either side of the icon stood a vase of artificial roses, an arrangement of silk lilies on a low table in front completing the lifeless ternion.

At the creaking of the door, I looked round to see a young policeman, gaunt and extremely thin, enter with a tray of tiny cans of soda and straws, standard fare for guests in Iraq, it seemed. As he smiled nervously from beneath a thin moustache, I noticed there was something wrong with his left eye, perhaps the result of an injury. I watched his delicate hands while he set the tray down on the polished wooden coffee table; the body beneath his dark blue uniform appeared so fragile I doubted he had the strength to do any real police work. We quickly finished the drinks and continued waiting, the shiny white air-conditioning units humming soporifically. Hassan and Ahmed wrapped up scrutinising the morning's photographs and began looking round the room before finally simply staring into space.

Eventually, the door opened again and our host arrived. Wearing a long cream *thobe* and a spotless white headscarf, or *ghutrah*, that extended below a generous waist, he walked towards us, dark eyes seeing everything. We stood up, clambering inelegantly out of our low seats. Speaking in Arabic, Omar introduced us to the man, who listened carefully and looked at us with polite interest. The thick brown beard, full cheeks and well-set figure belied his young years: he was not even thirty. The sign was given that we may sit down and, after he had carefully positioned himself in one of the chairs, Mazin Naif Rahim, local spiritual leader of the Mandaeans, began to speak. He addressed himself in Arabic to Omar while Hassan and Ahmed listened intently as, still toying with his mobile phone, the man talked about the people under his charge.

Some consider the Mandaeans to be the true descendents of the ancient Babylonians. Archaeological evidence points to their language – a form of Aramaic known as Mandaic – being the same as the dialect spoken in the cities of the Babylonian Empire, not only Babylon itself, but also Borsippa, Nippur and Uruk, all long since abandoned. The Mandaeans' system of astrology also resembles that practised in these once flourishing centres. It was Portuguese missionaries in the sixteenth century who first named them 'the Christians of St John' because followers of the Mandaean religion consider John the Baptist their saviour. Like all Gnostics, they shun the material world in favour of the spiritual. Not surprisingly, their main religious rite is immersion in water, which they consider a symbol of life. Rahim spoke for some time before stopping and waiting for the guide to translate. For a moment, Omar seemed to be collecting his thoughts, then he leant forward and began.

Rahim was spiritual head of the Mandaeans in Iraq, the leader of all followers of the religion, Sheikh Sattar Jabbar al-Hulu, having moved to Australia. The Mandaeans had lived in Mesopotamia for over two thousand years, he said, mostly in the area around the Shatt al-Arab and the lower parts of the Tigris and Euphrates. Glancing at Hassan and Ahmed, he explained that, since 2003, the population of Mandaeans had dropped by over 90 percent. Many had been killed, others had fled overseas or to Kurdistan because of violent attacks, forced conversions and harassment at the hands of radical

Islamists. Now, there were just some five thousand left. The Mandaeans' traditional work as goldsmiths and silversmiths meant they were targeted by criminal gangs and militias for ransoms, especially because, as pacifists, their beliefs forbade them from carrying weapons.

His eyes attentive beneath thick eyebrows, Rahim studied us while Omar described how it had become too dangerous and the water too polluted for the Mandaeans to carry out baptisms in Iraq's two great rivers. Instead, they had to use a special pool inside the building. With a gesture to the cross in the alcove, Omar explained that the *drabsa*, as it is known, was the symbol of the Mandaeans. Above the niche, the text inscribed in marble, he said, was taken from the 'Treasure of God', the Mandaeans' sacred book, the script being in both Arabic and the unique alphabet of the Mandaean-Aramaic language.

Rahim invited us to look at the baptism pool. We filed out of the long reception room and followed him along a passage to an area that resembled a small, half-finished spa, brightly lit by fluorescent strip lighting. Centre stage was a rectangular pool of rather murky water with steps leading into it along the length of one side and a large, very elaborate chandelier above. With an air-conditioning unit the size of a vending machine as the backdrop, the holy man stopped in front of a badly grouted wall bordering the pool and started to speak, looking at Omar and gesturing towards the opaque water. While waiting for the translation, I glanced round at the odd decor: marmoreal crazy paving, bathroom tiles, and filigree gold lamps on the walls. This was where the baptisms were carried out, began Omar, once Rahim had finished. Mandaeans believed multiple baptisms and ablutions washed away impurity from the body, and the more times they were done, the better, so the soul could pass on to the next world.

In the far corner of the room, I noticed a cloth canopy

suspended from bamboo sticks with a couple of simple wooden bench seats beneath. I picked my way over the tangle of pipes, hoses and cables that lay around to take a closer look. Between the two seats was a battered table with several large stone discs on it. Rahim followed me and, through Omar, described how this was where Mandaean wedding ceremonies took place, the bride and groom sitting on the thinly padded benches. A small olive sprig protruded rather sadly from between the bamboo and the canopy, a symbol, I imagined, to wish the young couple a peaceful life. For those who remained in the country, this felt to me like the triumph of hope over experience, the protection afforded Mandaeans appearing as effective as the flimsy construction of sticks and cloth before me. My attention drifted back to Omar, who was finishing by explaining that Mandaeans were only allowed to marry within the sect.

After browsing the various panels of writing and pictures that adorned the walls of the strange room, it was time to thank our host and leave. As we left the building, guarded by police, I wondered how long it would be before the rather elegant interior with its polished woodwork and marble would be reduced to the same state as the once splendid merchants' homes we had visited earlier.

We have just been for an evening walk through town, bright shop windows lighting up otherwise tenebrous streets. Omar told our police escort we did not need them and we slipped out into the dark with only the two plain-clothes guards, Ali the photographer, and Mazen, the grey-haired driver who, spending so much time behind the wheel, was keen to stretch his legs. We walked single file along the raised pavements in front of luminescent window displays and barber shops, looking at thin children buying sweets and swarthy men being shaved. Shops here that once sold music now peddle only recordings of Koranic verses, while the liquor stores have disappeared altogether, their Christian owners gone, or murdered. Omar said he had a headache and needed to stop in a pharmacy, so we ambled on without him, confident he would catch us up. As we paused to look at rows of biscuits and chocolate bars in an open shop front, a policeman emerged from the shadows of the street, the dark blue of his uniform as camouflage in the night. Like many in this country, he bore more than a passing resemblance to its former dictator. Black eyes flashing, his tone at first seemed merely curious, his questions just meaningless noise to the non-Arabic speaker. Only as Mazen and Ali tried to field his queries did I realise that neither of the guards was with us. The policeman's forehead wrinkled and his voice hardened with each successive question. Ali pointed to his camera and shrugged, a flow of words accompanying the gestures. As the policeman turned to the driver, the black truncheon at his waist catching the light, I asked Ali what was happening.

'Is OK,' he said, shaking his head. Ever tactile, he touched my arm in an effort to reassure me, but the look on his face had quite the opposite effect.

Idle passers-by were solidifying into a crowd, listening attentively to the man in uniform, looking at us, starting to jostle with each other. Nobody was smiling, not even our normally jovial driver. Cigarette still in his nicotine-stained hand, he took out his simple mobile phone, hairy fingers quickly pushing buttons, while Ali now turned his attention to deflecting the questions from the gathering youths. I saw Mazen dialling again and then again, trying to reach Hassan or Ahmed. His oversized Adam's apple rose and fell and his tongue passed over his lips. Perhaps because he had an audience, the policeman's tone was now sounding overtly hostile. He stepped forward, eyes narrowing: it was no longer necessary to understand Arabic. The tranquillity of the morning's boat ride suddenly seemed a world away. A microcosm of the Arab Street, it appeared, was now in front of us.

Then, as if having received stage directions, Hassan and Ahmed appeared, one from either side, nonchalantly reassuring the policeman with picture IDs that put him back in his place. I looked around: the crowd had dissipated and instead shoppers drifted as casually as before. Lighting another cigarette, Mazen had just begun talking to the two minders when Omar arrived.

'What was the problem?' I asked, as Hassan explained our encounter to him.

'He wanted to know where the security was,' said Omar, wiping his forehead. 'It's not a problem.'

We headed back in the direction of the hotel and soon found ourselves on the tree-lined corniche. In more liberal times, waiters in white jackets served cocktails at casinos here. Now, straggly bushes and uneven pavements spoke of poverty and neglect. Set back from the road, a statue, twice life-size, formed a silhouette in the dark evening air, one hand held in front. Clouds of moths and midges fluttered and floated round the dim streetlamps on either side and, in the distance, on the far bank of the Shatt al-Arab, tiny yellow lights twinkled. We approached the angular-faced giant and Omar translated the script on the square waist-high plinth beneath. It was Badr Shakir al-Sayyab, he said, a local man and Iraq's most renowned twentieth-century poet. Ali took a photograph for his collection, the flash quickly attracting two policemen who appeared from nowhere. Omar's papers from the Ministry and Hassan's ID card met with confused looks, shaking heads and an insistence that we move away from the statue and not take any more pictures. Fear is never far below the surface in Iraq: fear of making the wrong decision, fear of the hierarchy, fear of thinking rather than simply obeying.

We are in a bar a couple of hundred metres further along the corniche sitting on yellow plastic chairs, our soft drinks on the matching table in front of us. Groups of men sit a short distance away, talking, laughing, discussing and smoking as men do anywhere. The brightly lit bar, set between the road and the slow-flowing river, now black, is what passes for nightlife in post-war Basra. The air is warm and deceptively comforting as Hassan pulls out the magazine from his semi-automatic pistol before showing it me. He keeps a firm hold of the gun; I find it strangely reassuring that he trusts no-one. I look up and in the distance see the Ferris wheel, now a rainbow of colours lit up against the night sky, still turning languidly. I reflect on how Sinbad's fictional adventures ended happily with the sailor finding great wealth through 'fortune and fate'. Sadly, after all I have seen today, I fear that only the latter awaits the current inhabitants of this once flourishing city.

Babylon Revisited

I take another drag on the *shisha* and relish the flavour of double apple tobacco before blowing the smoke out, the scented cloud dissipating before my eyes into the warm evening air of the hotel courtyard. My gin and tonic is slipping down beautifully and, if Peter does not arrive soon, I shall have to order another. I pick up my phone from the table to check the time again: he should have been here half an hour ago. As I touch it, barely audible above the Arab lounge music, a huntsman's horn: I have a text message. Peter's taxi is just arriving at the hotel; I should order him a G&T. Sucking with satisfaction on the water pipe, I look for a waiter in the rapidly fading light. They are all so polite here, so willing, so helpful, so easy on the eye. I wish they were like that at home. I ask for two large gin and tonics – *Tanqueray*, please – watching his manicured fingers as he taps the order into the gadget he is holding. The badge on his chest says he is called Jamil.

No sooner has the waiter gone than Peter walks in. He sees me waving behind my veil of smoke and pads straight over. They have taken his bag up to the room, he says, flopping into one of the black faux wicker armchairs. We talk about his flight from London, the food, the delay, the taxi ride, until Jamil reappears with the drinks and sets them down on the table, together with bowls of nuts and spicy biscuits, flavours of the orient to whet our appetites. Our gins are delicious and just the thing to get us in the mood for our short holiday. I can feel the tobacco and alcohol going to my head, but the high starting to lift me into party mode is not induced by social drugs alone: it is simply from being back in Dubai, the sparkling city of hedonism where, if you are willing to suspend disbelief, you can imagine all your dreams coming true. Here is where you can experience the sensuous pleasures of the Middle East seemingly without limit, where you can indulge yourself in the delights of luxury shops and feast on your fantasies. Come to Dubai and leave behind all that guilt for, here, you can enjoy yourself without the faintest glimmer of a conscience.

We decide to dine at the hotel and ask Jamil for the menu. As he lights the tea candle in the glass on our table, I notice two young couples entering the patio and looking round for somewhere to sit. With their dark skins and close-cropped goatees, the men, like so many here, look straight from Arab central casting. I wonder if their polo tops really are a size too small or whether their muscles are simply too big. The women might have stepped out of a fashion magazine, a little white dress next to its electric-blue twin, long hair ready for a photo shoot, pouting lips shiny with gloss, doe-like eyes noticing nobody but registering everything. Perusing the menu, Peter asks if I am going to have a starter. I say I am, while I watch the men guide their high-heeled trophies down the steps towards one of the square tables. Jamil returns to take our order. As Peter plays with his signet ring and reads out his choice, I wonder how the waiter dresses when he is not in his burgundy and white hotel uniform, what sort of place he lives in when he is not dashing round the palm-filled patio, dutifully attending to the whims and desires of the well-heeled clientele. I imagine him commuting to a tiny apartment in some distant corner of Dubai on the driverless metro system built to ferry domestic staff and other people without cars around this sprawling city. He asks what we would like to drink. We order water and a bottle of wine, a 2010 Sancerre. It is all tapped into the little gadget.

The courtyard continues to fill up with a mix of expats and Gulf

State tourists. Tanned legs in designer footwear strut in front of black *abayas* that sweep along the floor, sky-blue shorts contrast with starched white *dishdashas*, and ice-cold beers gather condensation while steam rises from glasses of mint tea: the only things that mix are the cigarette smoke and the fruity fragrances drifting in billowing clouds from the *shishas*. Words of English, Arabic and French dance in the air while tambourines and traditional *ouds* shake and strum an exotic melody above the pulsating, sensual baseline of the electro-beat that pounds from invisible loudspeakers, a soundtrack to the scene. A teenage boy in an embroidered waistcoat and black harem trousers appears carrying a tray of hot charcoal. Using what look like sugar tongs, he quickly replaces the ash on the bowl of my water pipe with glowing coals. Sucking the mouth-tip, I take another deep drag on the pipe, savouring the taste of the smoke. Over the starter, we discuss what we would like to do in the coming days. We both know people here. I tell Peter he should meet my friend Cesar: we can go out for dinner together, perhaps party afterwards. We want to go shopping, but have no idea what we want to buy. The main course arrives and our conversation descends as fast as the wine in the bottle: we begin to discuss the people around us, who we find sexy, who not. We jokingly pair each other off with the most unsuitable partners, vying to see who can spot the least likely match. We are sliding into holiday mode. I can feel myself slipping into fantasy land.

Next morning, the smoke from the *shishas* has vanished from the courtyard, replaced by dazzling sunlight, but the dregs of gin and wine are still flowing through my veins. I am part way through my usual hotel breakfast routine: juice, then fruit salad, followed by smoked salmon and scrambled eggs. After the virtuous start, I feel less guilty as I tuck into a *pain au chocolat* and a blueberry muffin. Peter is wolfing down his own standard fare, which approximates a full English breakfast. We laugh about the night before. We have thought of things we need to buy.

After a slow start to the day, we stroll over to the Dubai Mall. It is only a few hundred metres to the world's largest shopping centre, but the walk in the early summer heat brings back vague memories of Camus' *L'Étranger* from French class, of scuttling along shadeless streets. The last time I was here, 'The Old Town' was still being built, a mass of cranes, hoarding, and sinewy workers from the subcontinent, armies of shadowy figures working through the night as we cruised past in our air-conditioned taxi. Now, we are in the middle of a copy of an ancient desert city that never existed, imitation mud walls concealing comfort and luxury, palm trees and lawns growing as if on hormones. We walk past a long, decorative pool in the broad courtyard of a five-star hotel that looks like a 1950s Hollywood film set. At the far end, feeling as if we have trekked across the entire Arabian Peninsula, we pass through heavy glass doors into the coolness of the Souk al Bahar where the first thing we see is a pastiche of an 'olde English tea shoppe', all ruche and pink swirls, with tapestry-style seat covers and curtains. It is like Barbie meets Miss Marple: it is hideous. We quickly realise the souk has about as much to do with a Middle Eastern bazaar as Selfridges on London's Oxford Street. There are escalators and air-conditioning, stands peddling souvenirs, shops selling fine furniture, and a store specialising in erotic underwear. Two mannequins in the window are clad in scraps of red and black lace, strategically placed love hearts providing the finishing touch. Al Bahar is compact and up-market, but its designer chocolates and couture scarves languish in empty boutiques. It is a soulless place in every sense of the word. We float through its corridors and out the other end, where we make our way over the bridge, a gentle arc that leads to where the real shops are.

Towering above us is the world's tallest building, the Burj Khalifa, a sparkling spire reaching over 800 metres into the sky. Separating us from this edifice is a large turquoise lake that spills out from the promenade in front of the Dubai Mall. A modest crowd, braving the heat and with cameras at the ready, has gathered at its edge. Suddenly, a mass of fountains shoots up, flamboyantly spouting water 150 metres into the desert air in time to music. A ripple of applause and gasps of amazement drift across from the crowd. On my previous visit, the Burj was half the height; now it stands a triumph of engineering. It is the latest example of a human fascination that began all those years ago in Babylon with *Etemenanki* – the 90-metre-high Tower of Babel; a fascination with constructing ever higher buildings, with reaching to the heavens in a demonstration of power, of invincibility. How apt that the shimmering skyscraper should stand in this of all cities, a glittering centre of hedonism. I stop to look at it, shading my eyes against the reflection of the sun on the water and glass. For a building containing a third of a million tonnes of concrete, it is remarkably graceful: few must be those, I suspect, who fail to be impressed at the sight of it. Peter hates heights, but I determine to go up the tower whilst we are here.

A few moments later, we have exchanged the dry, burning heat for the air-conditioned protection of the mall with its piped music, spacious atria and wide avenues housing over a thousand retail outlets. We meander along one of the walkways, strolling past some shops, wandering into others, enjoying their perfumed interiors. We feel fabrics, smell leather, look at watches, start to be tempted, all the time slipping deeper and deeper into the fool's paradise of consumerism, Dubai-style. We are as surprised to discover T-shirts selling for hundreds of dollars as we are to find stores like Topman, the latter no doubt catering to the expat market. Caucasians walk by, barely within the limits of the respectable dress code requested on the mall entrance doors, arms and legs exposed as if on a beach holiday in Spain. Yet they are invisible to the locals and visitors from other Gulf States in their flowing robes: heads never turn, eyebrows betray nothing and, unlike back home, none of the Muslim males here hiss comments about morality to Western girls as they walk past. Men in crisp white *dishdashas* and women in *abayas* made of the finest cloth saunter along the mall's avenues, the pedicured feet of both in footwear that would cost some people a month's salary, their watches and jewellery lifted straight from the pages of a *Financial Times* weekend supplement. Doing my best not to stare, I try to imagine the lives of these people. I remember the words of a German architect friend who works a lot in the region. He told me about the huge houses he designed for families in the Gulf States, explaining how the basements were parking garages, with the domestic staff lodged in windowless rooms on the level below the collections of luxury vehicles. I look at the wealthy Arabs passing me in the mall and wonder if they will return to such mansions to be waited on by humble workers emerging obediently from the subterranean depths. As I watch those around me, I realise that the vast shopping centre is in fact a great leveller in this highly stratified population. As much as anything, the malls are one of the few truly public spaces here. It is too hot to linger outside, but their air-conditioned walkways offer even those of more modest means shelter from the desert heat and an opportunity to take part in Dubai's dream world, if only vicariously.

We walk as far as Bloomingdale's, finally giving in to our credit cards' itch to come out of our wallets, before continuing to the Galeries Lafayette, each now with a large bag. We drift in and out of one store after another. The plastic gets regular airings, the purchases become more capricious. The shop assistants, many more from the Far East than the last time I was here, are unfailingly gracious and smiling, professionals at making us feel like visiting royalty, opening doors and wishing us a pleasant stay. Like hypnotic *djinn* doing a dance of temptation, the range, the choice, the novelty, all start to swirl around as we explore level after level of the vast mall, equivalent in size to fifty football pitches. In the middle of it all we find the Gold Souk, a collection of expensive jewellers' shops in a simulation of an Islamic courtyard. They are surrounded by stores selling the sort of bling you might find on any high street, and in the middle stands a row of would-be-quaint wooden carts flogging cheap souvenirs. A few unrented retail spaces, their fronts covered by smart hoarding with Arabesque designs, lend this geographic centre of the mall a strangely unfinished feel. A sign at the top of an escalator points down to a basement branch of Waitrose, a high-end British supermarket. We trudge on past shoe shops and window displays of opulent furniture, a mass of golden swirls and purple velvet. We pause outside what claims to be the world's largest sweet shop and gaze at an Olympic-sized ice rink where children are skating, their excited cries echoing around the cavernous atrium. Shop after shop, boutique after boutique: the mall seems endless. We stop to admire the multi-storey waterfall with its silver statues of divers plunging its length, have a late lunch in a mock French bistro, and shuffle round the aquarium, knocking people with our shopping in the walkthrough tunnel as we watch sharks swim overhead.

If the coolness of the air-conditioning cannot temper our feverish acquisitiveness, fatigue and the increasing weight of our bags do. Eventually, we take a taxi for the journey back to the hotel, even though it is just a stone's throw away, and deposit our mass of purchases in a corner of the room, our homemade altar to consumerism somewhat spoiling the elegance of the minimalist Arabesque decor. Exhausted, but still feeling the benefits of retail therapy, we decide to relax by the pool and head downstairs to the striped sun loungers. We order cold Lebanese beers from a pool attendant with teeth as dazzlingly white as his hotel-issue polo top and discuss our plans for the evening. While Peter, the brim of his new baseball cap pulled low, checks office e-mails on his phone, I text my architect friend Cesar, reflecting on how Dubai must be heaven for someone in his profession. Cesar is a party animal and will show us a good time, I tell Peter between refreshing swigs of *Almaza*. A few seconds later, the sound of the hunting horn proclaims his response: we should head up to the Marina for drinks at the Yacht Club, followed by dinner. Peter contacts François, a mutual French friend of ours here, proposing he join us. François is a great fan of Dubai who is constantly encouraging us to come and visit. His reply does not come straightaway and sounds odd when it arrives. He will join us, but is not in much of a party mood.

A few hours later, our taxi pulls up at the Marina, a hot spot for expats at the other end of town, twenty kilometres away from our hotel. As we walk up the steps to the Yacht Club, I can feel perspiration already starting to trickle down my back in the humidity. We make our way to the bar past beautiful twenty- and thirty-somethings poised in the lobby like models in a brochure from an up-market clothing store. We quickly find Cesar. Like us, he has just arrived and has not yet been engulfed by the loud mass of party goers. His shirt, open at the neck, reveals a tanned chest, the rolled-up sleeves, muscular arms. I take an instant fancy to his blue suede loafers. We fight our way to the bar and, after some polite jostling, eventually manage to order beers. Everyone seems to know each other. Cesar greets and is greeted as we push our way through the crowd, trying not to spill our drinks. We go outside on to the terrace with its view of the Marina and lavish residential towers. It is almost as busy as indoors, but, again, the humidity is stifling. By now, I can feel my new shirt sticking to me. We fight our way back inside, but it is difficult to hear ourselves think above the music, the laughter, the voices. Finishing our drinks, we decide to go to dinner.

Peter texts François, who says he will meet us in the restaurant.

Another cab ride past a forest of skyscrapers, their countless windows lighting up the night, and then the three of us are sitting at a table for four in a South American theme restaurant that looks like a cross between a prison and a ranch. Brick walls and iron bars, cow skins and black and white photographs make a strange combination, but it works. While we wait for our Parisian friend, we order *caipirinhas* and a bottle of sparkling water from the Brazilian waiter, who makes a point of telling us that his name is Eduardo. With his slicked-back hair, he looks like Rudolf Valentino, but the Chinese symbols tattooed on his forearm place him firmly in the twenty-first century. We enjoy the air-conditioning, study the menu, say cheers when our glasses clink and sip our drinks as lounge music mixes with the conversation of other diners. Behind the long counter, a barman with a ponytail and a crooked nose is juggling three spirits bottles as he tries to impress two blonde women perched on high stools. They are laughing coquettishly, encouraging him and relishing the attention; above the music I can just make out their broad Yorkshire accents.

François arrives, escorted to the table by another waiter who, like Eduardo, is dressed entirely in black. I am shocked to see how much weight François has gained and struggle to stop my gaze drifting towards his newly expanded belly. We go through the greeting ceremonies and introduce him and Cesar to each other. Sitting down, he also orders a *caipirinha* and we, having nothing left but melted ice to sip noisily through our little black straws, ask for the same. Like Cesar, François is an architect, but, in contrast to my Lebanese friend, he is pale, his blond features and blue eyes sensitive to the city's glaring sun. Passing slender fingers over his dense flaxen beard, he tells us in his light accent he has had a bad day. In fact, he has lost his job, he sighs, just as the waiter returns with our order. We pick up our glasses, unsure what to say, stirring our cocktails with the straws. Then we drink and ask François to tell us what happened.

Things had been difficult for some time, he tells us: a colleague did not like him. The guy was an Emirati, so had the upper hand – they always do, he says, staring into his glass, eyes glistening. Foreigners here count for very little. If you are caught speeding you have to pay a huge fine, but locals do what they want, he shrugs. He says the colleague was jealous of him because he was producing better results. It did not take long for him to conjure something up, to plot a way to make sure François was sacked. Now, he needed to find a new post, fast, otherwise he would be thrown out of the country. When I ask whether he will get any compensation, he affects a laugh. He has to work thirty days' notice and then he has the same period again to find a job before losing his residency permit. The waiter reappears, beaming like a game show host, and asks us if we are ready. While the rest of us say what we want, François, biting what is left of his thumbnail, quickly scans the menu, then tells the waiter he will have a steak.

While I savour my *caipirinha*, Cesar says he knows a firm that might have some openings coming up. François seems unconvinced, but, quickly finishing his cocktail, appears to reconsider and thanks him for the lead. I study them as they exchange telephone numbers and agree to speak the next day. Our French friend becomes suddenly more upbeat, the sombre tone that had descended evaporates and, by the time the food arrives, we are all back in party mode and in need of more drinks. We order some wine, start eating and then Peter and I begin to list all the things we bought in the mall. By the time dinner is finished, it no longer seems to matter that François has lost his job and, after another bottle of Bordeaux, we decide to go to a bar that Cesar knows.

Once again, we are in a taxi cruising along the Sheikh Zayed Road, the multi-lane highway that forms Dubai's backbone, this time heading back south to the Marina area. The wailing strains of a Pakistani woman accompanied by unmelodic music warble out from the dashboard. As if transported to another world by his compatriot's voice, the silver-templed driver appears oblivious to us being in the car. Or perhaps he is simply tired: his thin body seems lost in his shirt and trousers and looks too thin to have any energy reserves. I wonder for how long he has been working today and whether he will fall asleep at the wheel. François is wide awake and laughs at everything, whether it is funny or not. I suspect he had been drinking before he joined us in the restaurant.

We pull up outside an entrance with well-built doormen in black suits and a queue of wannabes behind a thick red cord. As Cesar heads straight to the front of the line, I feel we ought to have arrived in a smart limousine rather than a yellow cab. I turn to look at Peter and François, hoping the young architect will be able to walk in a sufficiently convincing straight line to be allowed into the club. Cesar seems to know everyone in this city and a word from him is enough for us to be waved inside by the bouncers, guys over 1 metre 90 with boxers' noses, coiled earpieces dangling from cauliflower ears, and all the charm of henchmen in a James Bond film. The cinematic theme continues inside with ultra-modern decor of shimmering metal and white leather, like something from a 1970s sci-fi movie. Everyone is tanned, beautiful, dripping in jewellery. I expect a photographer from a society magazine to appear any moment to take pictures of groups of fashionistas with toothpaste smiles, eager to get their faces into the right glossy publication so everyone will see how happy they are. As we push through the crowds, a party of girls are just vacating a couple of sofas, clambering to their feet on towering heels and picking up glittery designer clutch bags. We sit down, Peter and François on one sofa, Cesar and I opposite. My Lebanese friend waves a waiter across. We have to almost shout the order above the pounding oriental electro-pop. I think I hear François saying it is the first time he has been here. He looks around at the clientele, so many of them working hard to sparkle, to look their best. People have a short shelf-life in Dubai; perhaps it is the heat. A brunette in an expensive-looking grey mini-dress strides over to Cesar and bends down to kiss him, taking care not to spill her glass of white wine. He stands up and for a while they chat before she looks across at us and smiles a cold 'Hello' between glossed lips. I watch her index finger trace a path across his stomach, fuchsia nail varnish vivid against his white shirt. A tray of drinks arrives and she kisses Cesar goodbye before blending into the crowd. It is impossible for the four of us to hold a conversation above the music. I chat to Cesar next to me, now and then glancing across to the others where Peter is nodding and frowning while François is talking incessantly and giving the occasional Gallic shrug. I suspect he is going on about his lost job again and worrying about the future. The alcohol has done its work, first relaxing him, then bringing euphoria, before finally casting him adrift into melancholy. I ask myself what he will do if he cannot find a new position here soon. Cesar touches my arm, his fingers warm. I have not been listening to him. Apologising, I say I am tired. As he crosses his legs and leans towards me, the blue shoes catch my eye again. As if reading my mind, Cesar smiles and, asking me if I like them, taps my leg with his foot.

I look at the Downtown area below me, the low-rise clusters of beige buildings interspersed with tufts of green. I think about François' tears after we left the club and his disappointment when Cesar's lead did not work out. Time is running out for him, disappearing like sand between his fingers. Every day counts. I realise that the brand of capitalism that has transformed the desert coastline into a strip of glittering glass and steel and turned burning sand into stylish oases operates with ruthless efficiency. The excellent service we experience everywhere is not because people here are better or nicer: they are frightened of losing their jobs at the snap of a manicured finger or the nod of a head and, with it, their work permit. Dubai is a work-hard, play-hard world: it is just that for some there is very little play, only toil.

Seen from up here on the 124th floor of the Burj Khalifa, the lake below now resembles nothing more interesting than a spilled energy drink. The Address, the fashionably white 43-storey hotel on its eastern edge, looks like a maquette; in the foreground sprawls the quarter-pie shape of the huge Dubai Mall. Beyond that, amidst the haze and dust, rows of skyscrapers, no longer towering, just a series of rectangles and tubes protruding from a distant, sandy surface. Down on the ground, it all seems so perfect, so sparkling, so solid, but from up here I get a real sense of the fragility of the fabricated world below. Just beyond the spectacular and sumptuous buildings of Dubai's new Downtown area lie the endless sands of the Arabian wilderness, a hungry beast waiting to strike when its prey is not looking. Like a long finger, the Burj Khalifa's thin shadow extends way beyond the city into the desert, as if taunting it. As I look out over Dubai, I am struck by the vulnerability of life here: the air-conditioned bubble with its flowing water, fresh food, greenery and comforts is completely energy-dependent. The entire city strikes me as being akin to a spacecraft with an artificial life-support system. From half a kilometre above the ground, I finally realise both the greatness of the achievement of creating this metropolis in the desert and the sheer folly of doing so. The Emirates are, I am told, the most unsustainable country in the world. From the observation deck of the Burj Khalifa, skilfully marketed as *At the Top*, it is easy to see why.

For all its riches, I doubt this modern-day Babylon will be

remembered a hundred generations hence. Despite its reputation for hubris and hedonism, the original Babylon was a great centre of culture and art. Somehow, I do not think the statues of divers we saw in the mall will one day find themselves displayed next to a section of the Burj Khalifa in the way that the stele bearing the laws of the Babylonian King Hammurabi stands in the shadow of the Ishtar Gate in Berlin's Pergamon Museum. Looking out from the observation deck platform, I wonder whether, in some future, tourists will visit the ruins of Dubai as I once did the remains of the fabled Mesopotamian city. Or whether, in two thousand years, there will even be anybody here to do the remembering.

And, reflected in the unsustainability of the city that stretches before me, I see the tenuous nature of my own presence here, in this country, in this holiday fantasy where you forget the value of the local currency, live for the moment and begin to believe that a new life could be created here instead. You can only suspend disbelief for so long. Only now does the reality of the situation become apparent. My return to Dubai puts into sharp focus how little has changed since my last visit, despite all my efforts to the contrary. I turn and walk towards the elevator, ready to go back down to earth.

In God's City

Struggling for breath under the weight of expectation, I looked at the clock on the dashboard, I looked at my watch, I looked at the time on my mobile phone: their verdict was unanimous. There would be no escape: the moment of truth was approaching inexorably. We had been in the traffic jam for what seemed like a lifetime, the silver strip of the Mediterranean on the distant horizon having long since disappeared from view. Gone were the fertile landscapes of the plain and in their place stood tired, dusty bushes struggling to survive in the increasingly arid environment. The air-con battled audibly to keep the temperature in the car to a bearable level while outside the glaring sun burnt as though determined to roast us alive. I imagined the car's tyres sticking like chewing gum to the asphalt as we inched forward. The road climbed, climbed, ever upwards, towards the interior, towards the city, as if we were ascending to the gates of heaven itself.

My chest tightened as I said we had to pull over and stop so that I could make a call. I clambered out of the car into the searing heat and walked safely out of earshot, not realising that the traffic and closed windows rendered my conversation inaudible anyway. I called up the name from the phone's address list, braced myself and pressed 'dial'. I could feel my heart beating as the call went through; I wondered if I was going to be sick. I prepared myself to attempt normal speech when I heard the voice on the other end. We spoke. No, there was no news: I would have to call back later. The anguish was to be drawn out a few hours more. A mixture of foolish relief at not having to face reality swirled dizzily with the horror of waiting yet longer before knowing one way or the other. It was as though the delay, the judgement, the sentencing, was being dragged out: a foretaste of the punishment to come. Nothing is worse than not knowing, than doubt: it is in uncertainty that the greatest fear lies.

I got back in the car. We did not say anything about the call. My friend is good like that. He can be very discreet. Perhaps it is something in the character of Swedes. We rejoined the traffic crawling up the hill to this most ancient of cities. I wondered what it would be like. I had heard it can change you. I had read of people who had been transformed by it, who had become religious, who had been overwhelmed by the experience, who had undergone an epiphany, who had gone mad. I wondered what the city would do to me.

Finally, we saw the reason for the delay: three wrecks of twisted metal surrounded by emergency services' personnel blocked half the highway. Statistically, more people die in road accidents in this country than from all the shooting and bombing. We negotiated our way past police cars and men and women in fluorescent safety jackets until, finally, we were free. We left the slow-moving river of traffic behind us, the road opened out and suddenly we were speeding towards the city. It was not long before we reached the outskirts. I was surprised by how high up we were and by the mountainous nature of the landscape. A modern development of little box-houses clung like limpets to the side of a barren hill. I should have expected it, but this was not how I had imagined it to be. I reflected on all that these homes represented as we pushed on towards the centre. We had arrived in Jerusalem, a place I shall never forget.

We drove around the Old City on a wide ring road with traffic lights, shiny road signs and dazzling white lines on fresh tarmac, an incongruous display of modernity and apparent normality in this crucible of tradition and the irrational. Eventually, we turned off and headed down a series of narrow, winding roads into East Jerusalem before arriving at our home for the coming days, the iconic American Colony Hotel. Originally a pasha's palace, it stood in a lush oasis of green, a veritable Garden of Eden with palm trees offering welcome shade, bougainvillea bursting with colour, and the gentle fragrance of jasmine, redolent of so many romantic fables.

Inside, the dark wooden reception counter, heavy furniture and colonial style decor made me think Hercule Poirot could appear at any moment sporting a white suit, straw hat and spats. While we waited to check in, I perused the hotel's brochure. The building had been bought at the end of the nineteenth century by a group of American Christians, it explained, and had begun life as a hotel in the early years of the last century, evolving to become one of Jerusalem's landmarks. The brochure claimed the hotel to be a haven of neutrality being owned neither by Muslim nor Jew, but, as I wandered round the foyer and saw the titles of the books for sale in the glass cabinets, I realised that, sadly, in Jerusalem there is no such thing as impartiality. Formalities concluded, we went to our room and unpacked. I sat on my bed and looked round at the antique furniture and the black and white photographs on the walls. Through the French windows the pool flashed turquoise, a reminder of the merciless sun outside.

Having come so far, I felt obliged to explore the Old City, but needed to do so on my own. After just a couple of minutes' walk from the hotel, I found myself in a rather shabby commercial street with shops selling mobile phones, shiny grey suits, haircuts, fruit, and vegetables. Drivers with thick, hairy arms dangling from the windows of Japanese cars hooted impatiently in the heat and dust as shoppers wove their way through the crawling traffic.

The street opened on to a wide road on the other side of which stood the Old City and the imposing sixteenth-century Damascus

Gate built by the Ottomans. Even as other, darker thoughts churned at the back of my mind, it was impossible not to be filled with a sense of wonder at the sight in front of me. I imagined Nabataean merchants arriving at the city, their camels laden with frankincense and myrrh, and, centuries later, crusaders leading one of the twenty-three sieges to which Jerusalem has been subjected over the years. For millennia, this city has occupied such a key place in human history that today its name is almost a part of the DNA of every Jew, Christian and Muslim, wherever they are in the world, observant or not. Now I, too, was here to see and experience Jerusalem, but my communion with the city was to be a bitter one.

Along the busy road outside the walls, tourists and the faithful, vendors and shoppers mingled in a noisy, chaotic melee, the visitors in awe of the sight ahead, the locals no longer noticing its crenellated fortifications and towers that stretched in front of them as they busied themselves with carrying, buying and selling all manner of merchandise, just like innumerable generations before.

In the footsteps of countless millions, I passed through the Damascus Gate and headed down the sloping stone slabs that led into a warren of alleyways and a street level of times gone by. I found myself absorbed into the Arab Market, transported to another world. Stall after stall lined passages so narrow that you could easily touch wares hanging on either side. Toys, scarves, cosmetics, tin pans and underwear: a kaleidoscope of gaudy tat crowded in from left and right. Ragged awnings kept out not only the sun, but fresh air too: the smell of spices, cheap perfume and perspiration swirled in an intoxicating and suffocating mix. Stout women in long nylon robes and *hijabs* paused to inspect the goods on offer and then pushed their way past me as if I, the infidel, were invisible. This market held none of the cultural or architectural attractions of souks I had seen elsewhere in the region and certainly none of the charms: it was a confusion of stifling tunnels 'Made in China', from the oppressive heat of which I could not escape fast enough.

I emerged somewhere near the Via Dolorosa where signs pointed the devout and the curious in the direction they were expected to take to follow the path Christ walked carrying the cross. I turned off and quickly found myself in a different, scruffier world with children playing and litter piling up in the corners, the cocktail of smells in the souk now replaced by the acrid odour of urine. A thin, ginger cat surveyed me nervously before abandoning its scraps and hurrying away. Generations of sandstone walls towered above, the once elegant mixed with a jumble of later add-ons, although 'later' is relative in Jerusalem. I continued walking, wandering, exploring and almost inevitably ended up at the Church of the Holy Sepulchre, steered perhaps by some invisible hand that guided me through the maze of narrow stone streets and cobbled alleys.

Built on the site of an earlier pagan temple, the church rose in front of me a mass of sandstone surrounded by more of the same, squeezed into the centre of the Old City. Two windows, each set in a high arch supported by thin columns, looked down on me like startled eyes. Beneath them was another pair of arches, one bricked up, the other a black rectangle – the gateway from the dazzling daylight to the shadows of the twelfth-century church. It is reputedly the spot referred to in the Bible as Golgotha, the setting of the crucifixion, which was outside the then city walls. It is one of those places you are compelled to enter. Inside, I was bewildered by the medley of separate churches vying with each other for the attention of the devoted and, presumably, the grace of God. Judging from the decor, gold seemed to be a key element in their argument. This place should have felt holy, but it was just touristic. Meditation and prayer might have been appropriate, but, despite the subdued light, there was no sense of peace amongst the jostling crowds, the shoulder bags with tour operator logos, the bouffant hairdos in artificial orange, white and black framed by headscarves. I recalled the brawl between Armenian and Greek Orthodox monks from two of the six churches that control the shrine and wondered how they would justify their behaviour with their hero's call to 'love thy neighbour'. Miraculously, I found a spot away from the shuffling masses whispering in countless tongues and sat down. I thought of the phone call. I thought about the situation. And I felt a deep sense of despair.

After a while – I do not know how long – I got up and went back outside to face the heat and the bright sunlight, the same sun that shone down on the Canaanites, Greeks, Romans and Byzantines when in turn they each ruled the city. I continued towards the Jewish Quarter and soon found myself in tidy streets where Orthodox men wrapped up in black coats and felt fedoras, despite the heat, chatted with each other, and boys with side curls and arms full of books walked purposefully to their *yeshivot*, their religious schools. Star of David flags hung from windows, limp in the afternoon heat. I slipped into a side street and after just a few paces was surrounded by almost rural stillness where only the occasional glimpse of washing drying on a rooftop line or a well-tended pot plant outside a door hinted at the area being inhabited. The sense of timelessness was palpable. Turning into an alley, I saw two gnarled olive trees before which a small sign announced that they were an estimated two thousand years old. I paused and contemplated the tumultuous past of the city and that these two trees, symbols of peace and already a thousand years old when the crusaders arrived, had witnessed and survived so much: the Romans and the Rashidun, the Umayyads and the Mamluks, the Ottomans and the British. Yet it was the fact that they might even have stood here at the time of the crucifixion that provided a living link to the past in a way a stone monument or a precious vase simply cannot. And their longevity put my own mortality into even starker contrast. I looked at my watch. The hour was approaching. I could feel my stomach beginning to writhe in anguish and my throat tightening as if gripped by an invisible executioner eager to carry out his task.

I drifted towards the Western Wall. As I ambled along a narrow, stuffy street, half a dozen American tourists scuttled past, their guards with handguns drawn. Did this make them feel safer, I wondered? I queued to pass through the airport-style security check and then walked out onto the Western Wall Plaza, created after the demolition of the Moroccan quarter following the Six-Day War. I pondered the wall's long history, the last two millennia of which have been as part of a ruin and, as I observed Jewish tourists around me, young and old alike, looking at it in awe, asked myself how people could attribute so much holiness to mere stones. And I wondered if there were not more important things in the world than fighting over rocks.

A discreet but all-pervading military presence was a blunt reminder of the strength of feeling the site engenders. Above, where the Second Temple had once stood, glistening in the sunshine was the Dome of the Rock, the ultimate symbol of the discord that lies at the heart of the city and that poisons the entire region. I wandered over to the wooden walkway that rose above the plaza to lead to the Temple Mount and a small Portakabin where more soldiers carried out further security checks, this time to make sure nobody was smuggling in Jewish prayer books or instruments, prayer by non-Muslims being forbidden within the boundaries of the compound. The openness and tranquillity of the Temple Mount proved a welcome respite from the suffocating labyrinth of the city below, but the ornately decorated Dome of the Rock itself, its golden cupola glistening in the sunshine, was strictly off limits to those not of the faith. Here, from the shady gardens of what Muslims call the Noble Sanctuary, I could see across to the Mount of Olives outside the city walls. Ironically, this most disputed site was the only place I had visited in the city that had any sense of serenity. I looked at my watch. It was time. I took out my phone and, with a sense of dread, dialled.

As we drove to Jerusalem, I had wondered what it would be like. Now I know. Jerusalem sits on a hill, a bastion of intolerance, its position inland symbolic of its isolation and of the stark contrast to the laic openness and modernity of Tel Aviv just sixty-seven kilometres away on the coast. Known, fittingly, as the navel of the world, it is the epitome of all that is regressive and inward-looking. It turns its back on the world and focuses its schizophrenic energy on how it can keep itself only for Jews, only for Muslims, only for Christians, each time to the exclusion of the hated other. It cannot, of course, fulfil all of these aims simultaneously. To me, it represents the abject failure of the representatives of the three great monotheistic religions to practise what they preach and an excuse for many others to barricade themselves behind the placards of bitter tribalism. Instead of love, tolerance, peace and forgiveness, the city encapsulates and exudes the antitheses of all its protagonists purport to espouse. If there is a God, surely he must despair when he looks down on Jerusalem.

Am I biased? Of course I am. In this supposedly holiest of cities, none of their Gods answered my prayers.

Afterword

While I was writing *From Souk to Souk*, the already volatile Middle East was swept up in the Arab Spring, dramatically changing the lives of millions of people. The media are filled with images of crowds filling the streets and accounts of revolutions. But when you have actually been to the countries and cities affected, watching events unfold feels very different.

Syria has been transformed from the country I visited. It used to be possible to walk the streets of central Damascus safely at night; now, by all accounts – in addition to the dangers brought by the fighting in the civil war – going out after dusk is a life-threatening experience as gangs roam the city. Aleppo, where I once contemplated the calm of the ancient citadel, has been the site of fierce fighting and large parts of the souk have been destroyed. Beirut's Place Sassine became a scene of carnage when a bomb went off and in Iraq the number of terror attacks is once more on the rise. Even Turkey has not been spared civil unrest.

It is easy to sigh and to dismiss the troubles in these seemingly distant countries as belonging to another world, one which does not concern us. Yet I hope that in *From Souk to Souk* I have been able to show a different side to life in these countries and that a common heritage links the lives of people around the globe to those of the inhabitants of the region, both past and present. The societies I encountered are in some ways markedly different from the one I live in, but my experiences have shown me that the aspirations and desires of the ordinary people are not so unlike our own.

Both on a cultural and a human level, the region covered in this book has an amazing amount to offer the visitor. With every visit, I learn something new, discover somewhere different and am continually impressed by the warmth and hospitality of the people.

And, in case you were wondering, all the postcards from Yemen arrived at their destinations.

Robin Ratchford
March 2014

Thanks for joining me *From Souk to Souk*!

If you enjoyed the book and have a moment to spare,
**I would really appreciate a short review – even just a
couple of sentences. You can go to my book's page on
Amazon if you scan this QR code**

Stay in touch:

www.robinratchford.com

Robin Ratchford on Facebook

@robinratchford on Twitter

.